Baby, you're going to love this collection of designs by Linda Gillum!

So the next time you hear the exciting news that a baby will be arriving soon, grab your cross stitch supplies and this leaflet and start stitching! From bibs and a bath set to wall hangings and an afghan, we've gathered 41 of Linda's best creations to honor these tiny bundles of love. The oh-so-precious projects are great for shower gifts or to celebrate your own new arrival.

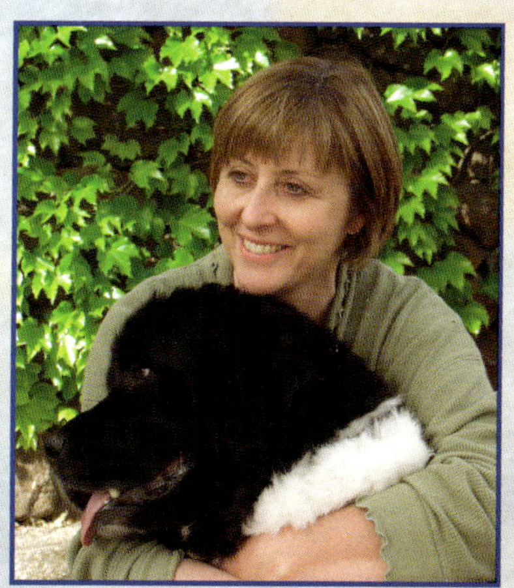

Well-known for her coordinated baby ensembles, Linda Gillum says she enjoys drawing baby designs because they're so cuddly sweet. "They're not too serious. They're fresh, new, and joyful." Linda is the executive vice president of Kooler Design Studio, Inc., a California-based company that is commissioned by needlecraft publishers like Leisure Arts to create a variety of needlework designs. Linda, who has designed since 1979, has a strong drawing technique as the foundation for her diverse style. Her favorite subjects to draw are animals. Her teddy bears are among her most sought-after designs. In addition to drawing, Linda likes dollmaking and figurative sculpting. She and her husband, Joe, also spend time remodeling their home. "Joe is a great guy! He's always so good about building things for me." Linda's constant companions are her three dogs — Newfoundlands named Cookie and Molly and a Labrador named Payton — who enjoy walks in the park, "helping" in the studio, and sitting in the living room while she reads.

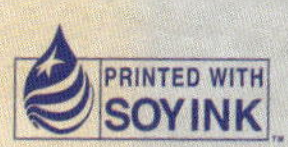

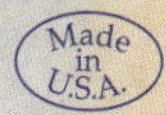

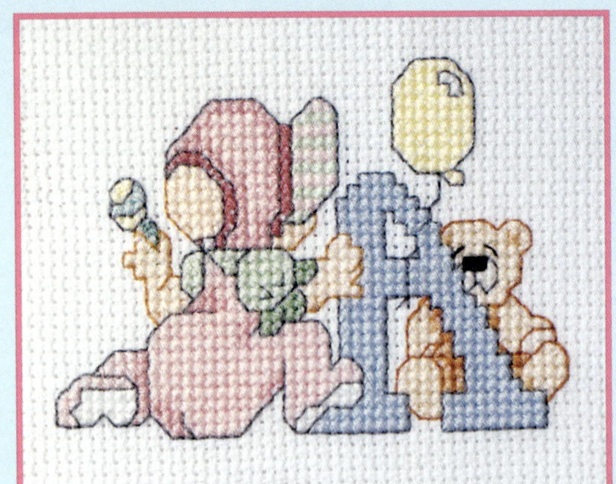
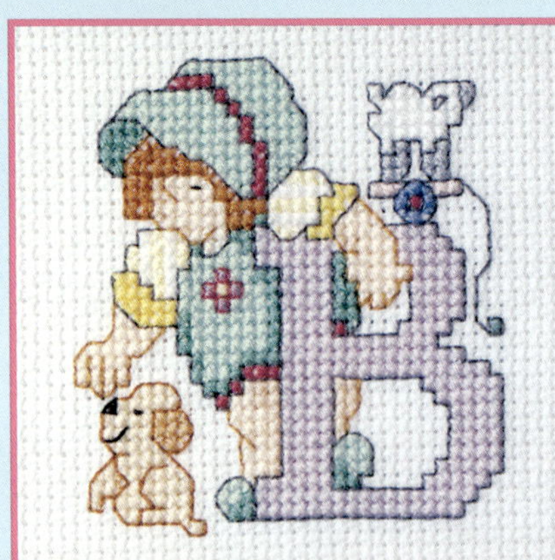
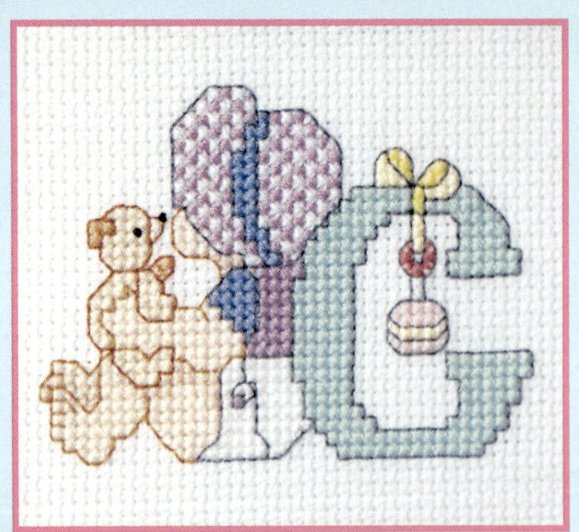

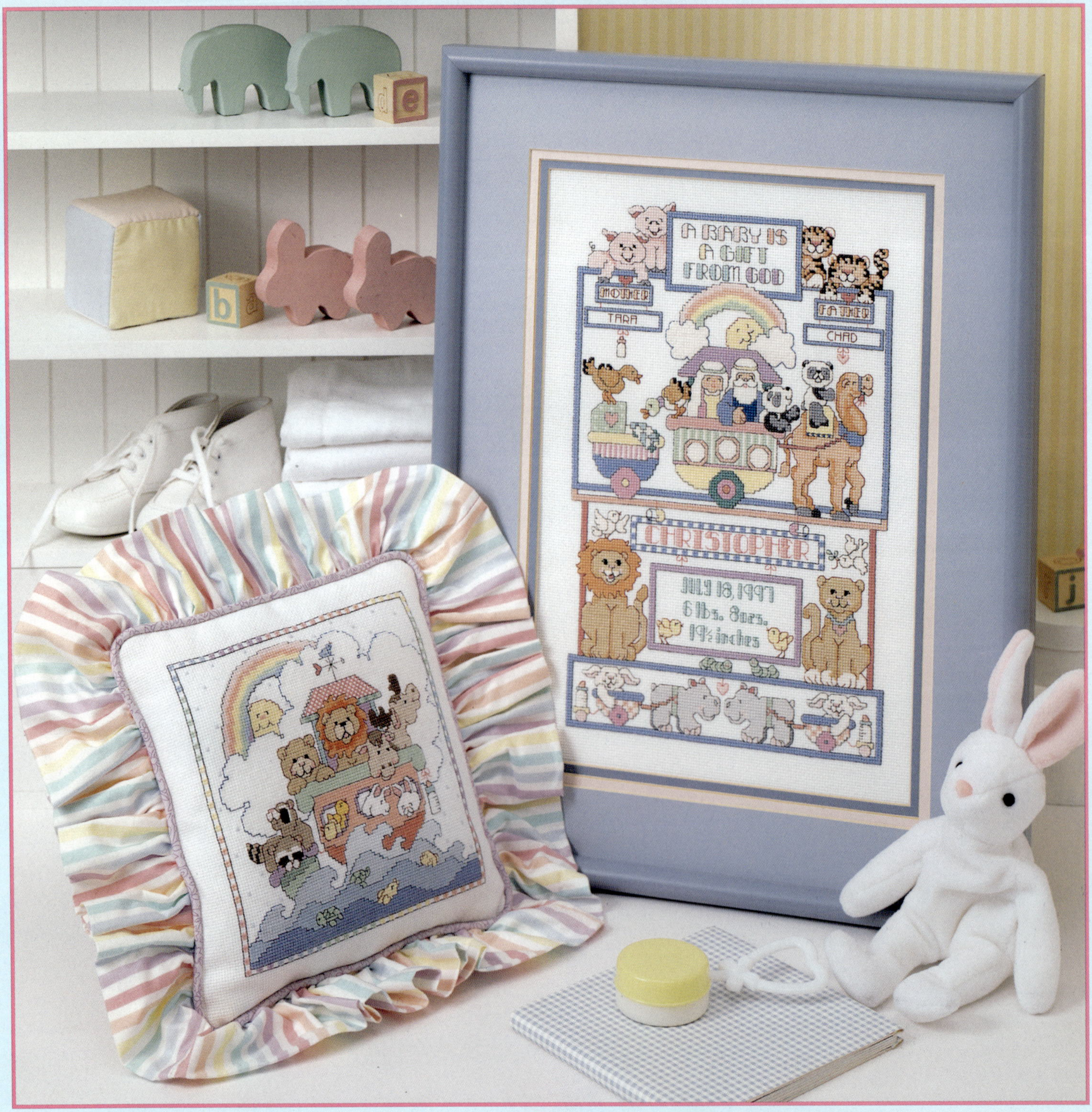

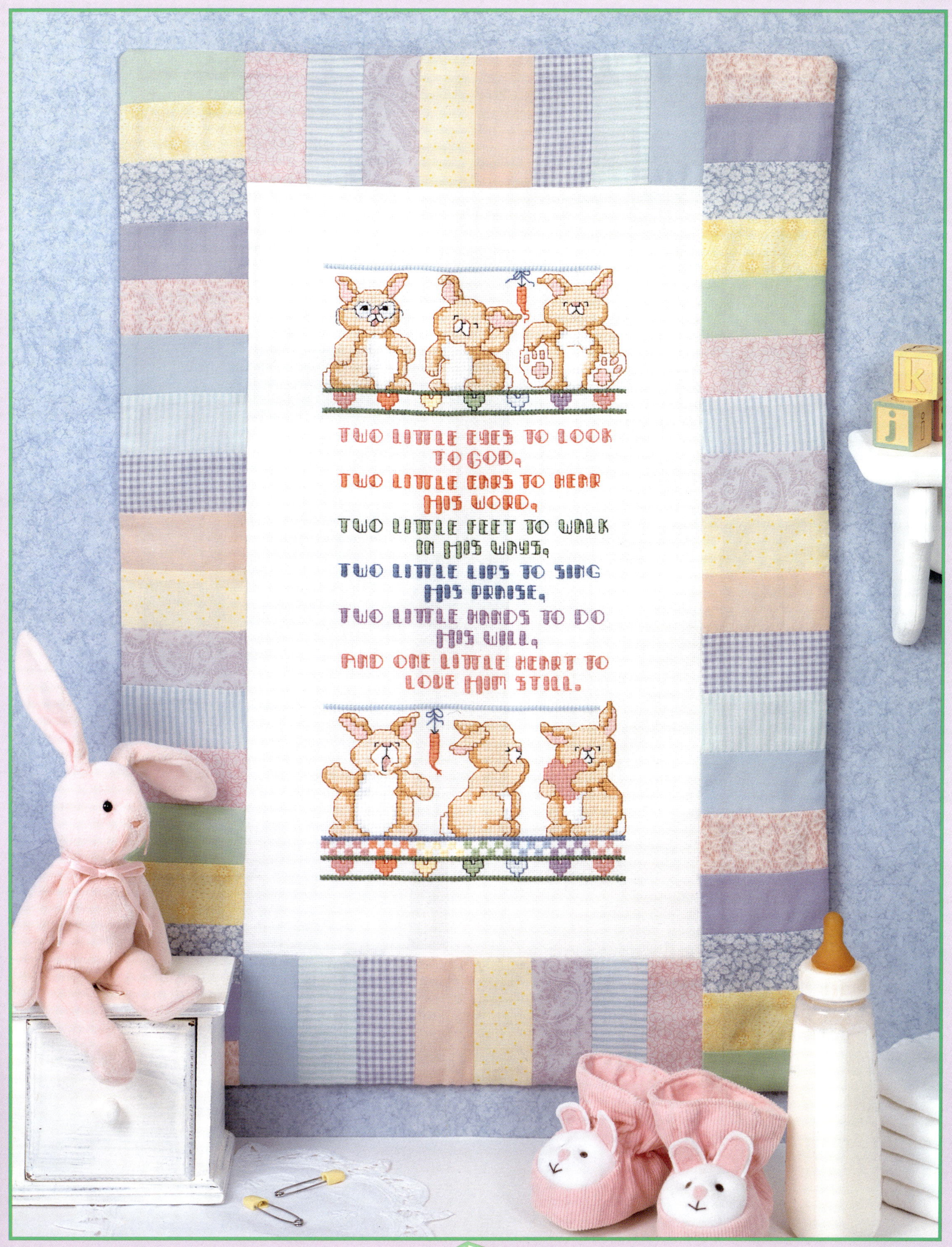

TWO LITTLE EYES TO LOOK
TO GOD,
TWO LITTLE EARS TO HEAR
HIS WORD,
TWO LITTLE FEET TO WALK
IN HIS WAYS,
TWO LITTLE LIPS TO SING
HIS PRAISE,
TWO LITTLE HANDS TO DO
HIS WILL,
AND ONE LITTLE HEART TO
LOVE HIM STILL.

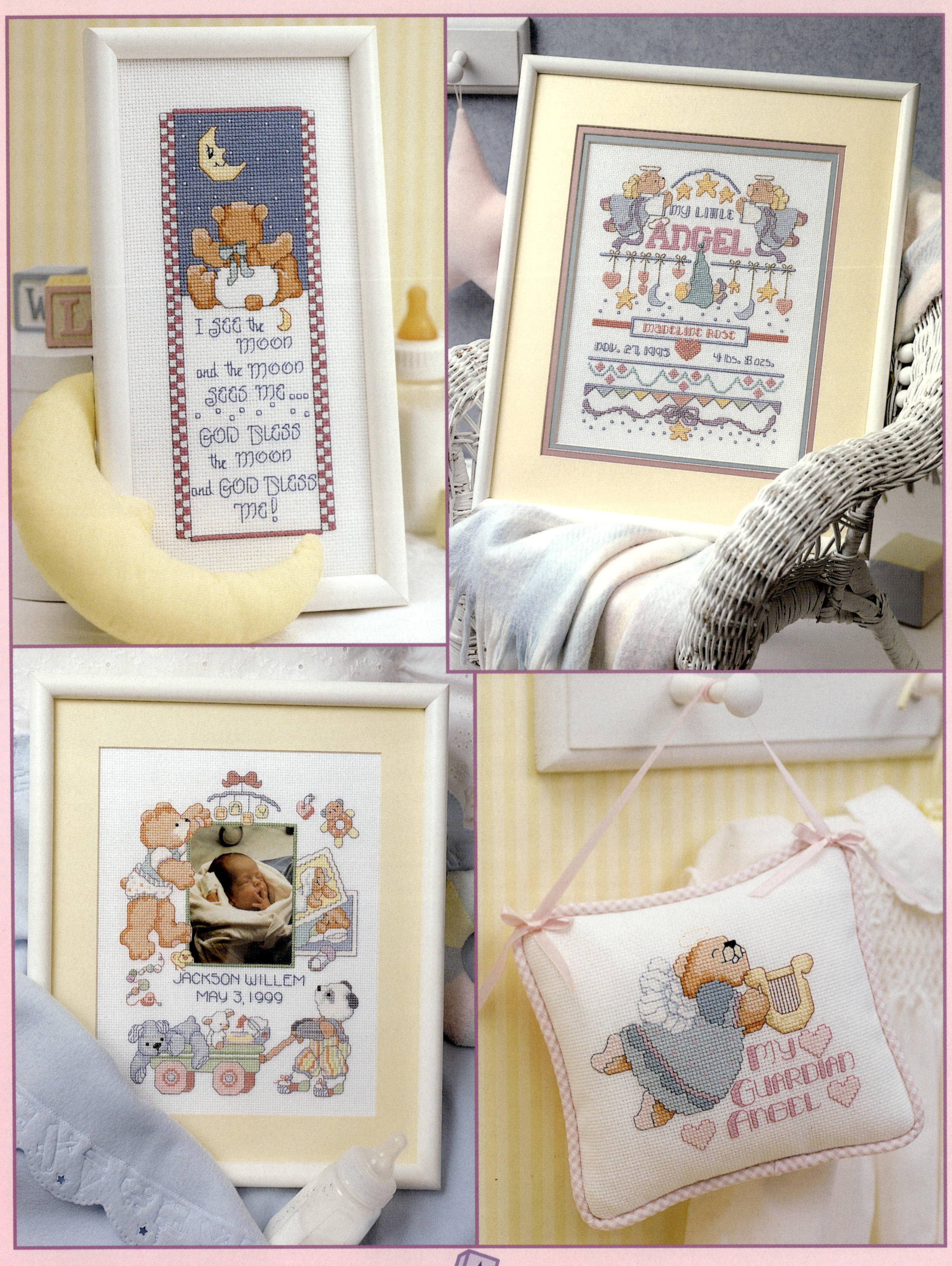
I SEE the
MOON
and the MOON
SEES ME...
GOD BLESS
the MOON
and GOD BLESS
ME!
MY LITTLE
ANGEL
MADELINE ROSE
NOV. 27, 1995   4 lbs. 8 ozs.
JACKSON WILLEM
MAY 3, 1999
MY
GUARDIAN
ANGEL

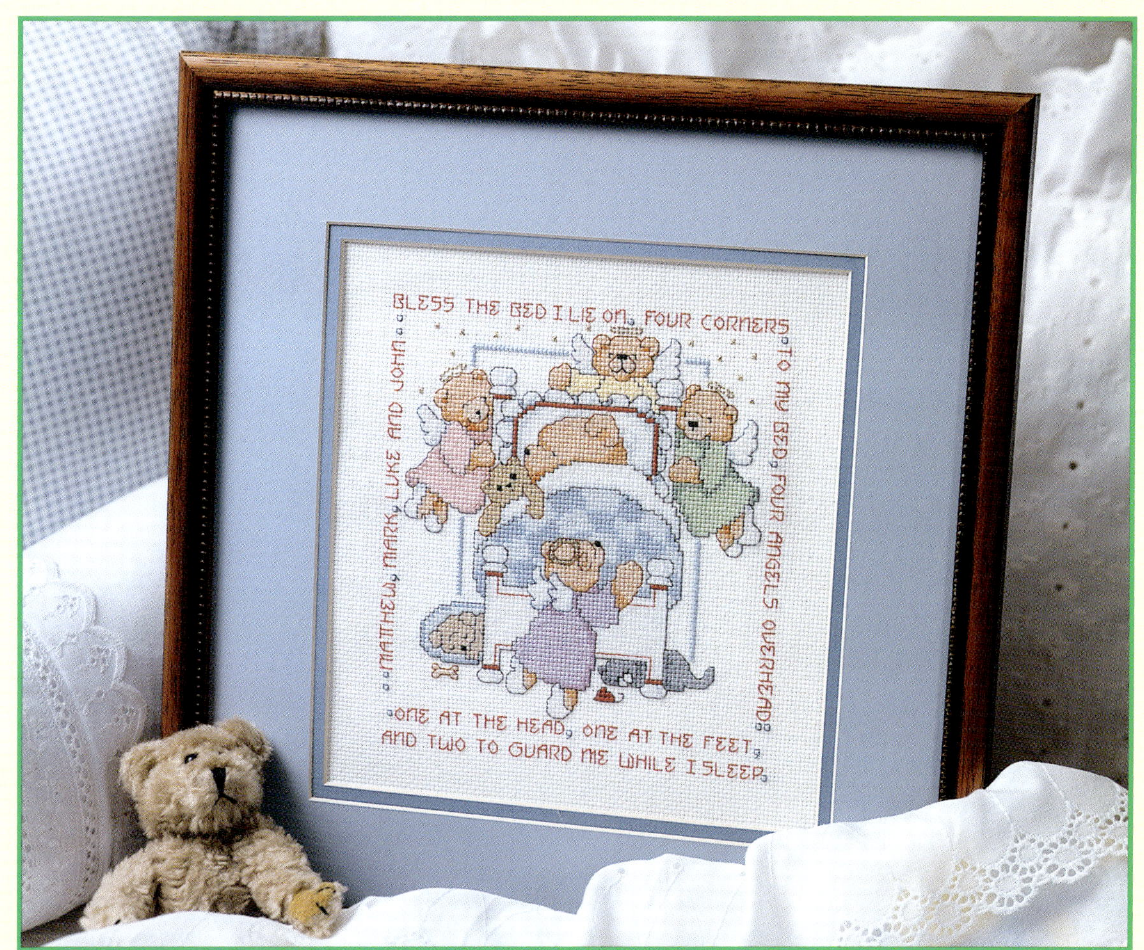

BLESS THE BED I LIE ON, FOUR CORNERS
TO MY BED, FOUR ANGELS OVERHEAD
MATTHEW, MARK, LUKE AND JOHN
ONE AT THE HEAD, ONE AT THE FEET,
AND TWO TO GUARD ME WHILE I SLEEP.

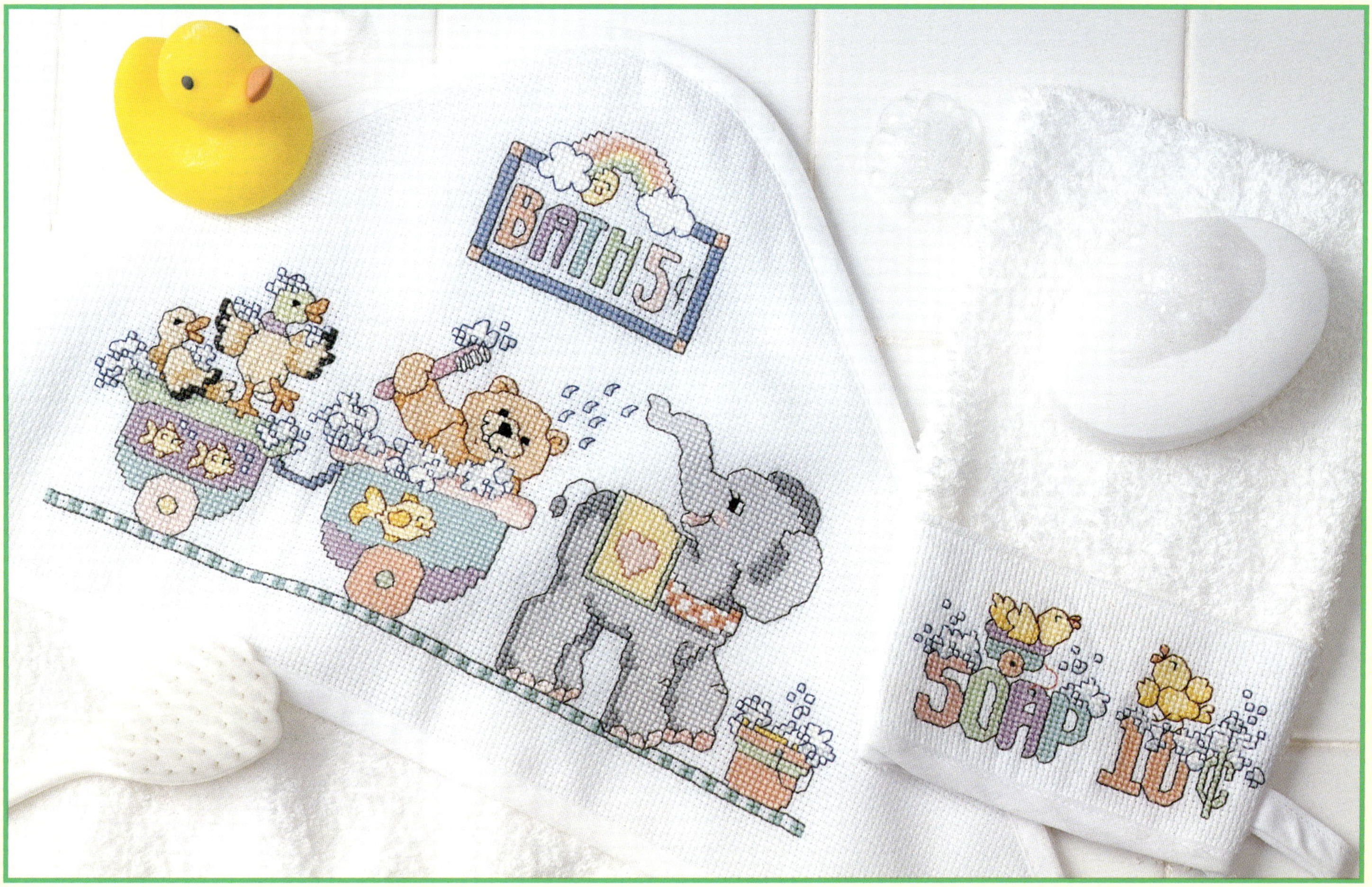

BATH 5¢
SOAP 10¢

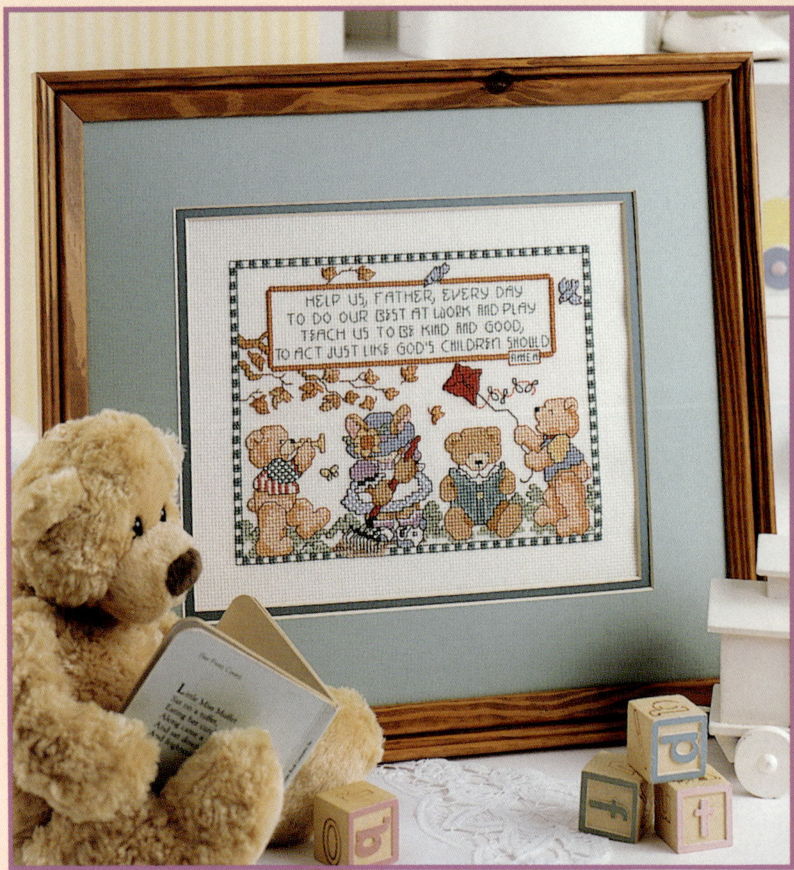

Help us, Father, every day
To do our best at work and play
Teach us to be kind and good,
To act just like God's children should.
AMEN

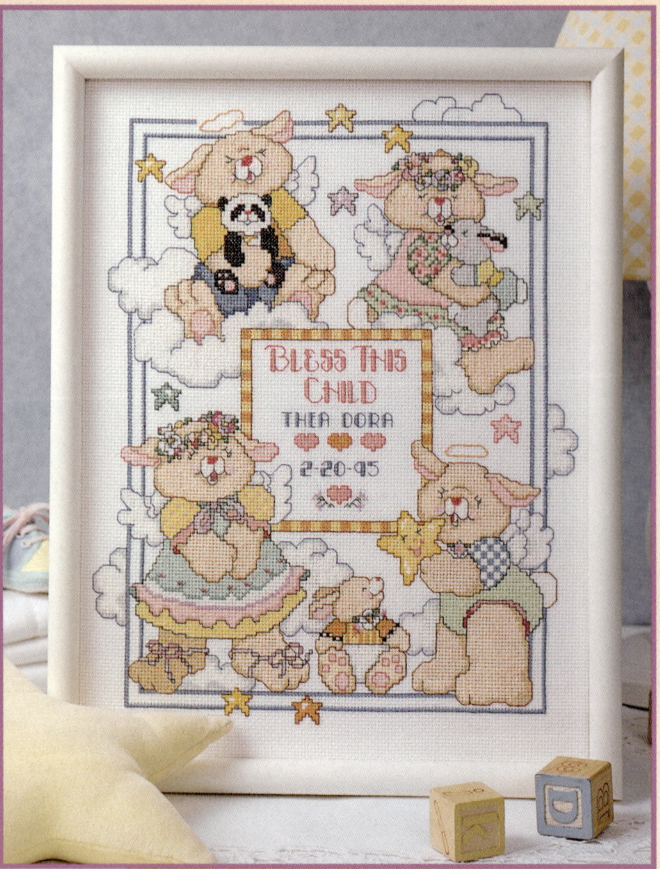

BLESS THIS CHILD
THEA DORA
2-20-95

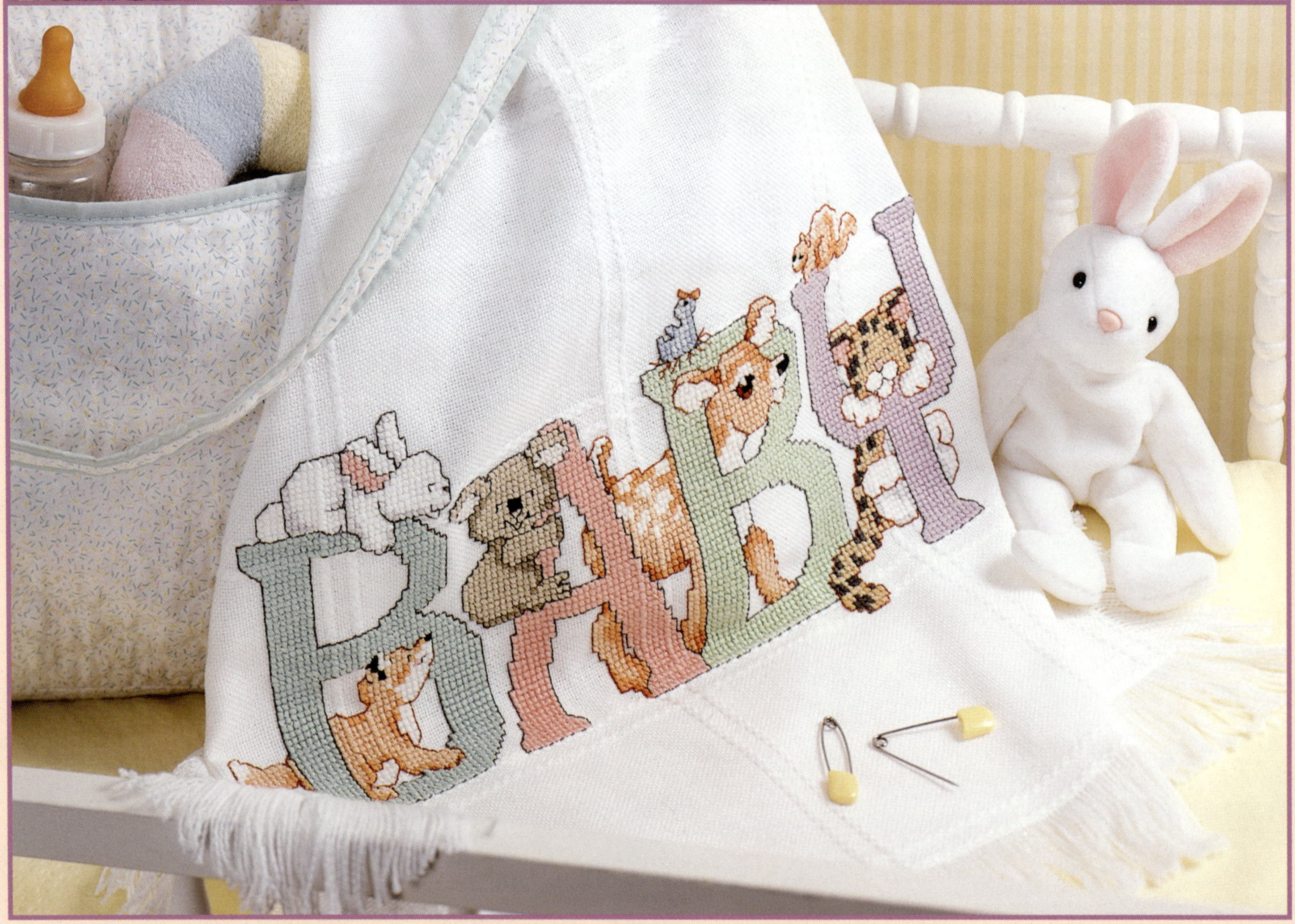

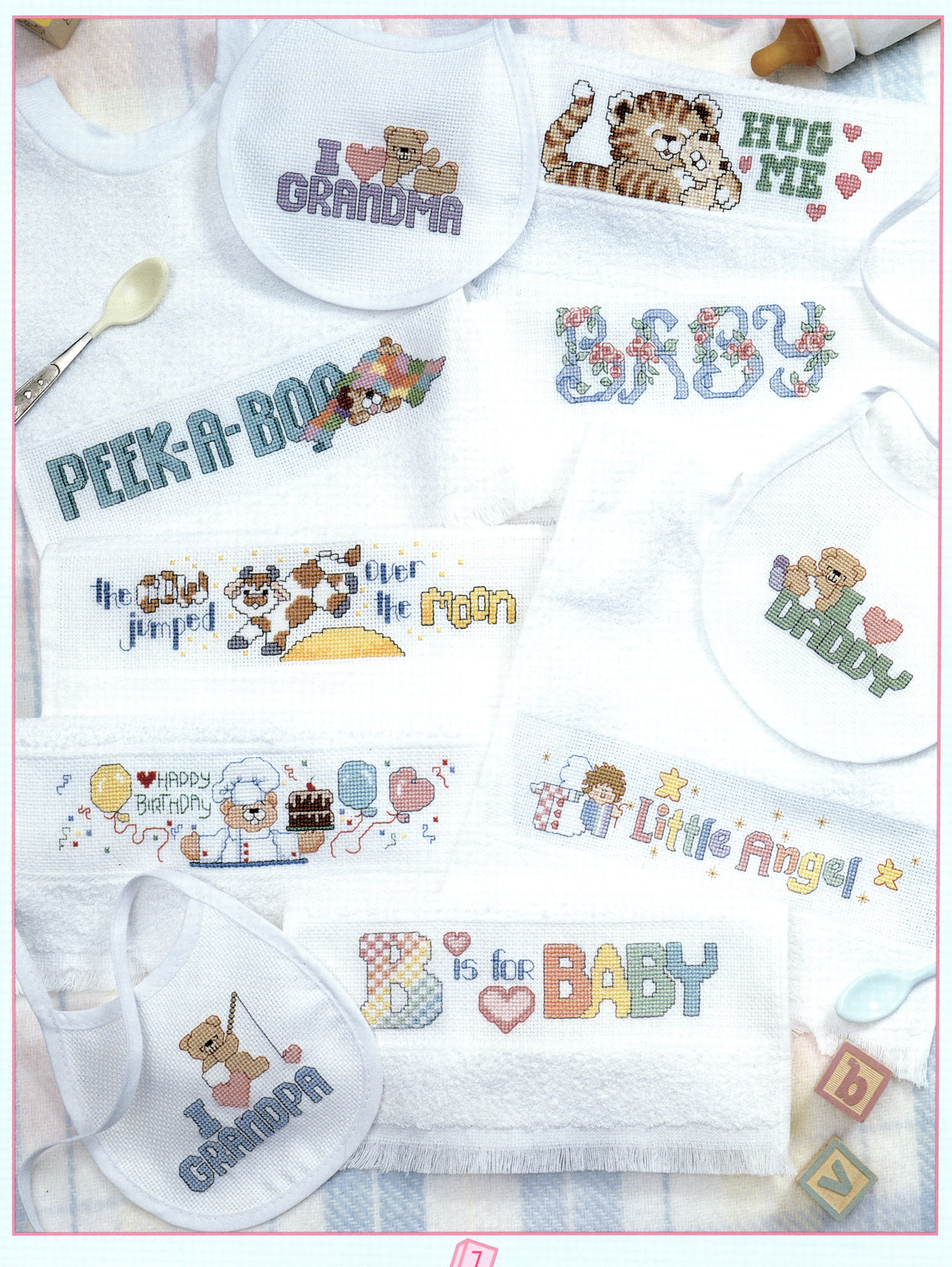

I ♥ GRANDMA
HUG ME
PEEK-A-BOO
BABY
the cow jumped over the moon
I ♥ DADDY
Happy Birthday
Lil Little Angel
I GRANDPA
B is for BABY

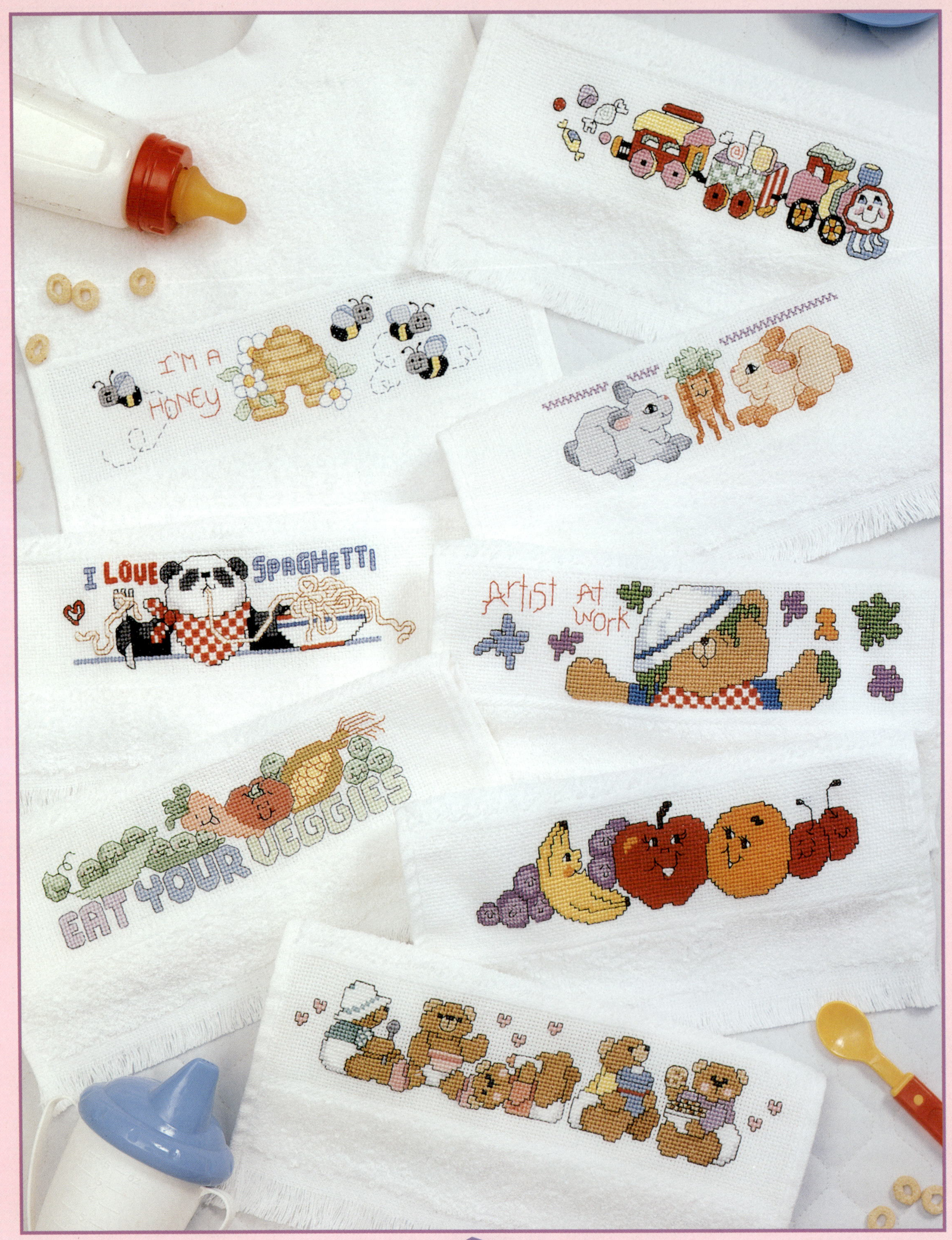
I'M A HONEY
I LOVE SPaGHeTTi
Artist At work
EAT YOUR VEGGIES

Cow (115w x 29h) • Bears (126w x 25h)

X	DMC	1/4X	ANC.
☆	blanc	☆ 2	
✖	209		109
∨	210		108
⊥	318	◣	399

X	DMC	B'ST	ANC.
H	334	✏	977
◆	349		13
✕	351		10
＼	352		9

X	DMC	1/4X	ANC.
◣	434		310
5	435		1046
+	436		1045
⊙	738		361

X	DMC	ANC.
◐	743	302
✧	744	301
⊘	762	234
✱	899	52

X	DMC	ANC.
=	951	1010
◥	958	187
$	959	186
▲	3341	328

X	DMC	B'ST	ANC.
2	3713		1020
♥	3716		25
Π	3755		140
■	3799	∕	236

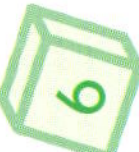

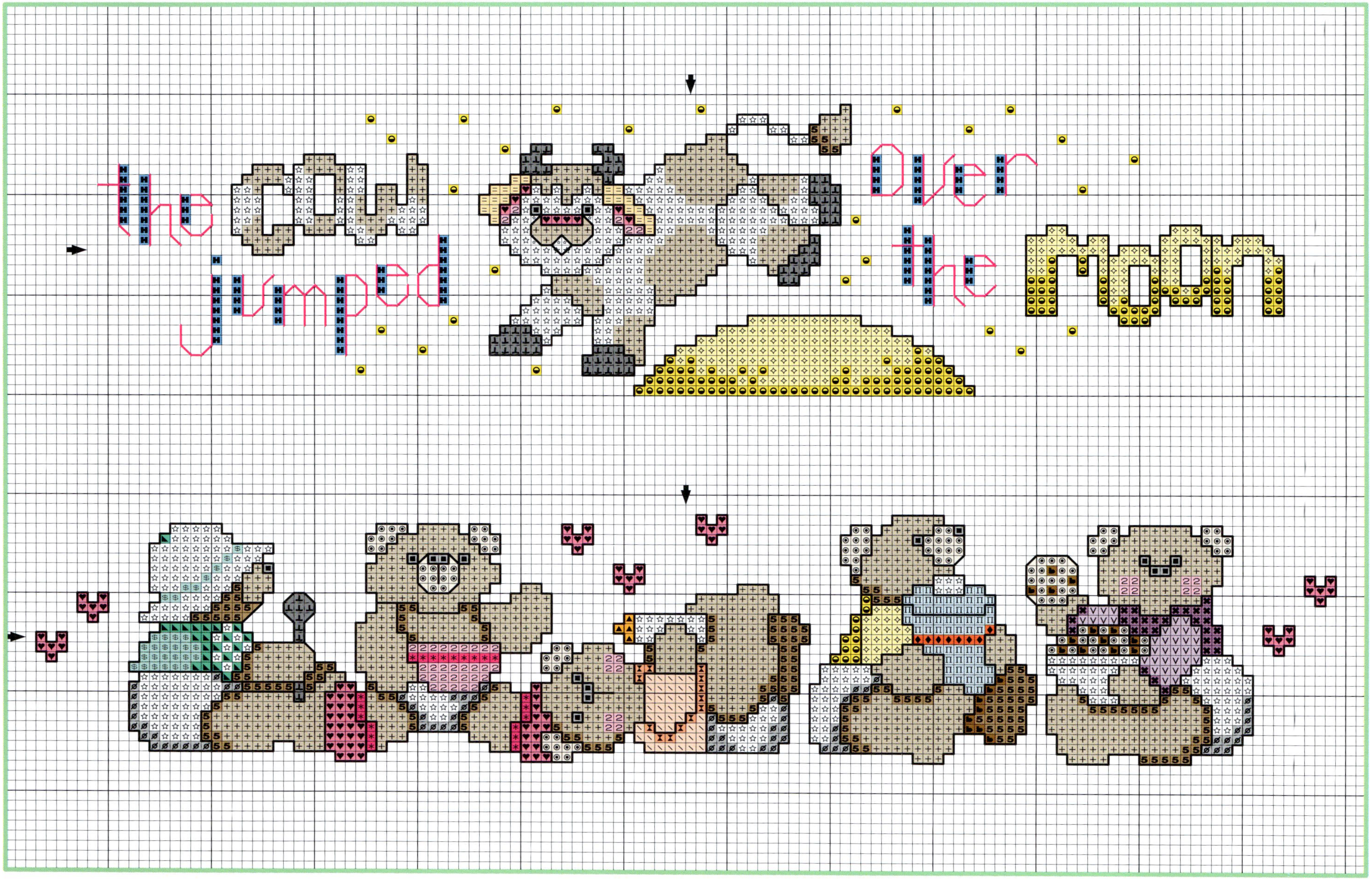

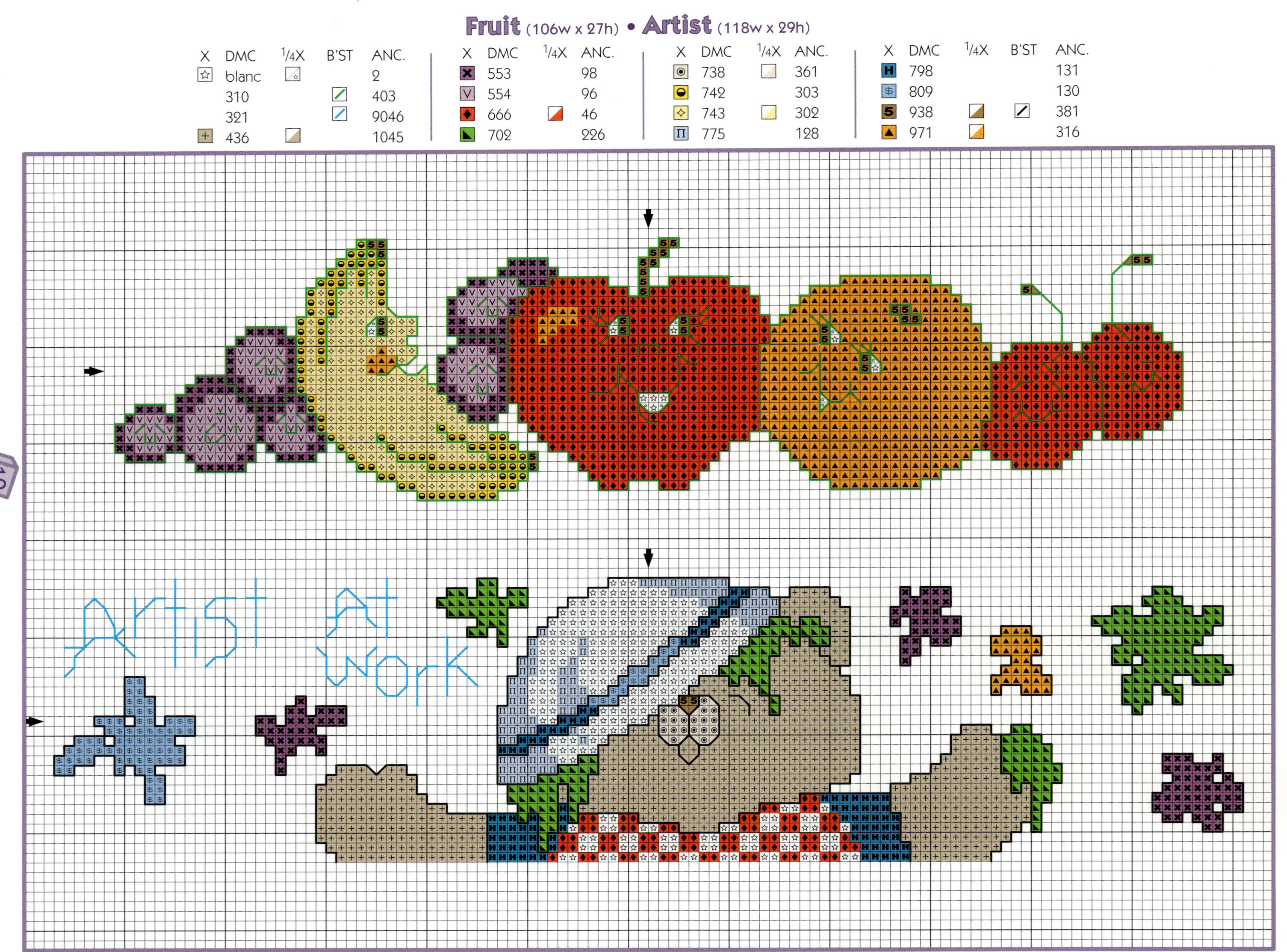

Fruit (106w x 27h) • Artist (118w x 29h)

X DMC 1/4X B'ST ANC.
blanc 2
310 403
321 9046
436 1045

X DMC 1/4X ANC.
553 98
554 96
666 46
702 226

X DMC 1/4X ANC.
738 361
742 303
743 302
775 128

X DMC 1/4X B'ST ANC.
798 131
809 130
938 381
971 316

Artist at Work

10

Train (98w x 25h) • Spaghetti (96w x 27h)

X	DMC	1/4X	B'ST	ANC.
☆	blanc	⬚		2
8	209	◩	◹*	109
2	211	◩		342
◼	310	◩	◹†	403
V	413	◩		236
	434	◩	◹*	310
✓	498	◩		1005

X	DMC	1/4X	B'ST	ANC.
+	606	◩	◹†	334
◿	666	◩	◹★	46
✳	712	◩		926
○	727	◩		293
◆	741	◩		304
d	762	◩		234
	798		◹★	131

X	DMC	1/4X	B'ST	ANC.
◉	809	◩		130
◆	913	◩	◹	204
▽	955	◩		206
♥	3608	◩		86
□	3755	◩		140
‖	3824	◩		8

* DMC 209 for candy. DMC 434 for spaghetti.
† DMC 310 for train, candy, and bear. DMC 606 for word and heart.
★ DMC 666 for candy. DMC 798 for wording.

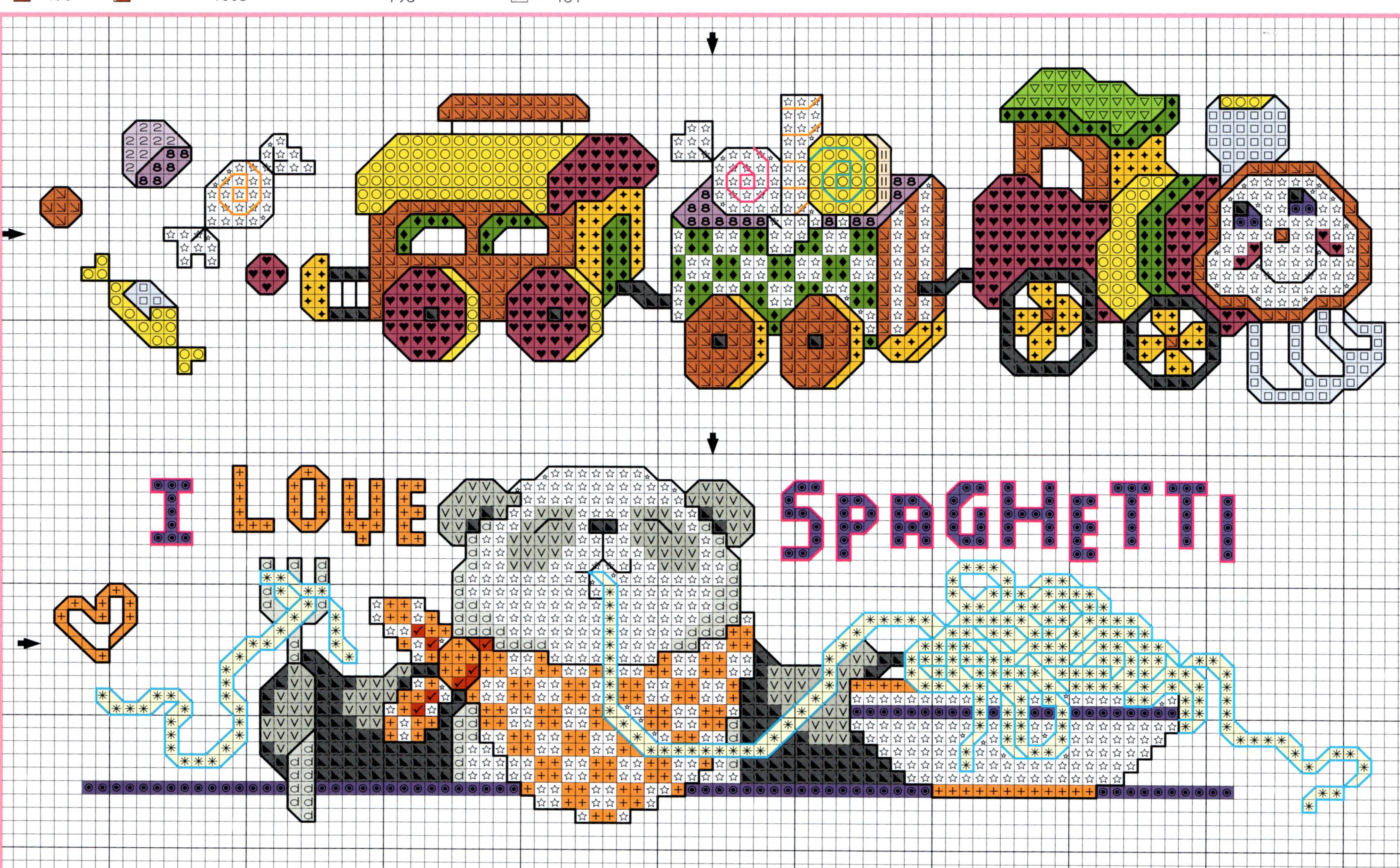

Happy Birthday

X	DMC	1/4X	B'ST	ANC.
P	3825	◨		323
Π	842	◨		1080
	911		★	205
%	912			209
◆	913	◨		204
H	921	◨		1003
d	945	◨		881
▷	955	◨		206
♡	964	◨		185
8	3325	◨		129
¢	3776	◨		1048

Bunnies

X	DMC	1/4X	B'ST	ANC.
☆	blanc	◨		2
Σ	209			109
	301		*	1049
■	310		†	403
	317		★	400
	335	◨	+	38
2	340			118
T	402	◨		1047
◐	414	◨		235
✻	415	◨		398

X	DMC	1/4X	B'ST	ANC.
4	433			358
◆	606	◨	*	334
/	712	◨		926
◇	739	◨		387
+	744	◨		301
✕	762	◨		234
□	775	◨		128
◇	776	◨		24
◎	799		†	136
	801		+	359

*DMC 301 for bunny, carrots, and bear. DMC 606 for strings, confetti, and cherry.

†DMC 310 bunnies, carrots, bear, and cake plate. DMC 799 for clothing and confetti.

★DMC 317 for balloons. DMC 911 for carrots.

+DMC 335 for noses. DMC 801 for cake.

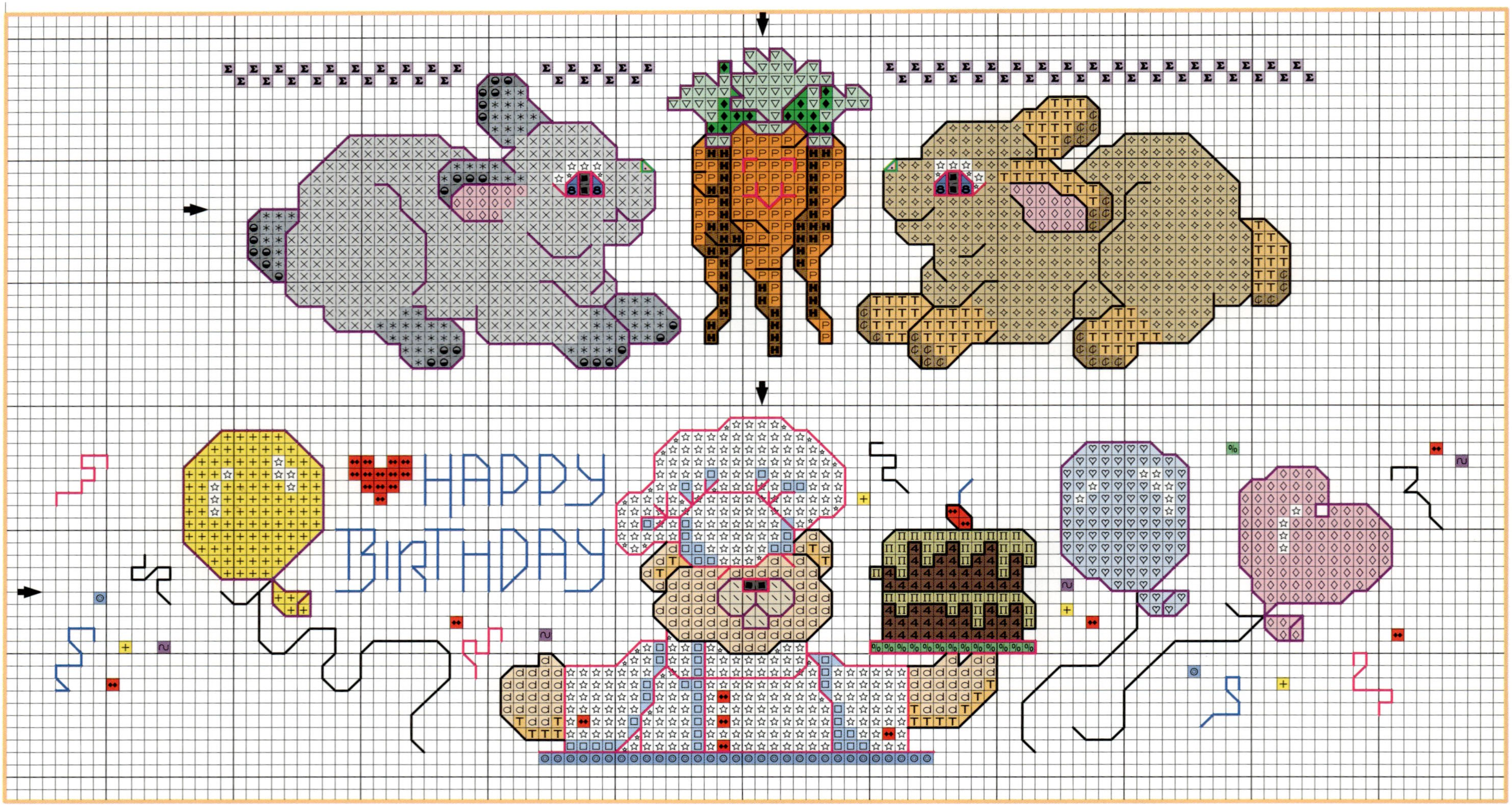

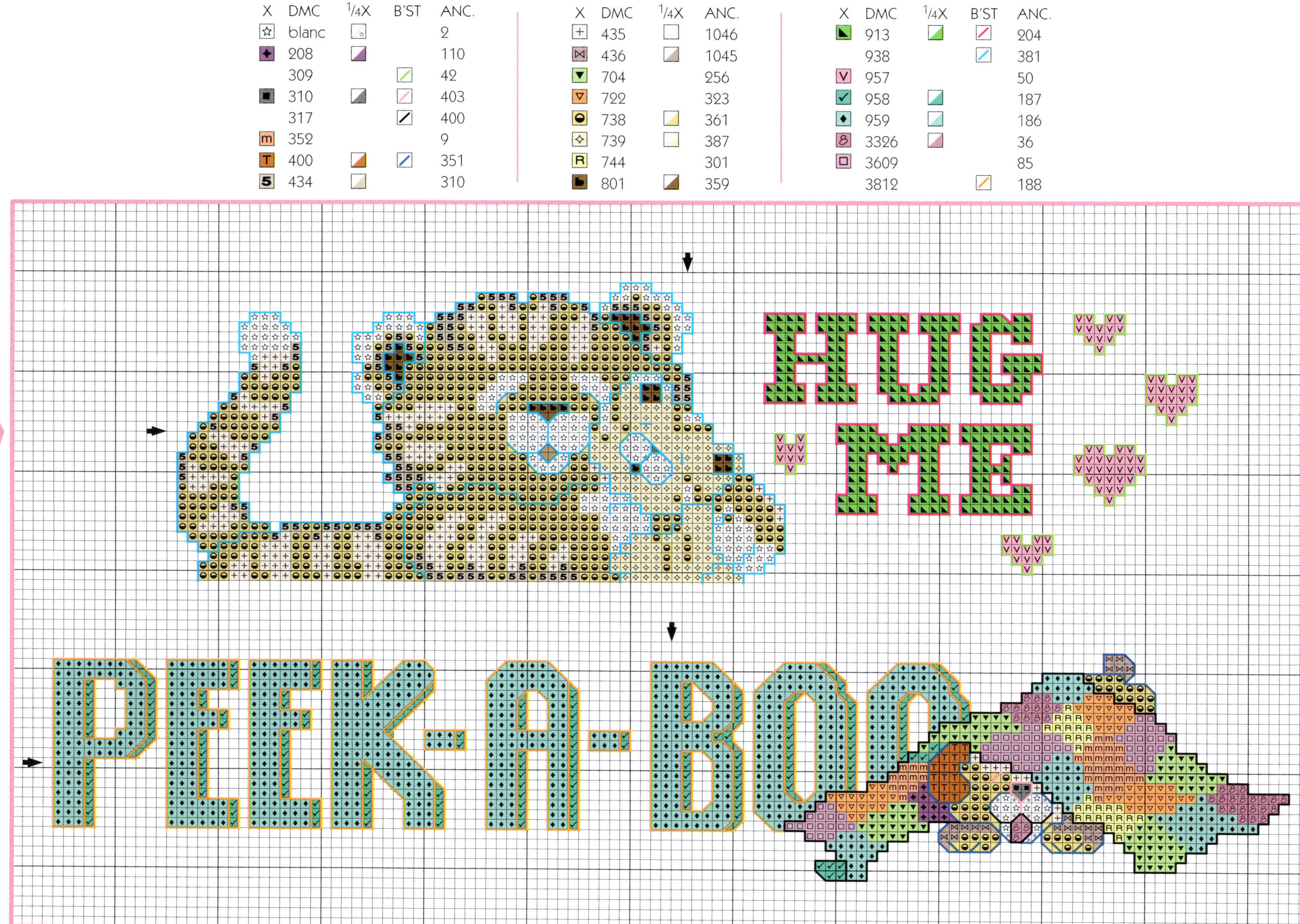

X	DMC	1/4X	B'ST	ANC.
☆	blanc	☆		2
◆	208			110
	309			42
■	310			403
	317			400
m	352			9
T	400			351
5	434			310

X	DMC	1/4X	ANC.
+	435		1046
⊠	436		1045
▼	704		256
▽	722		323
◒	738		361
✧	739		387
R	744		301
■	801		359

X	DMC	1/4X	B'ST	ANC.
◢	913			204
	938			381
V	957			50
✔	958			187
◆	959			186
8	3326			36
□	3609			85
	3812			188

B Is For Baby (99w x 26h) • Little Angel (115w x 26h)

B Is For Baby (99w x 26h)

X	DMC	1/4X	B'ST	ANC.
☆	blanc			2
+	211			342
	301			1049
	334			977
	335			38
	347			1025
	414			235
►	729			890

Little Angel (115w x 26h)

X	DMC	1/4X	ANC.
+	744		301
m	800		144
✧	818		23
2	951		1010
◁	955		206
□	964		185
★	3326		36
◆	3824		8

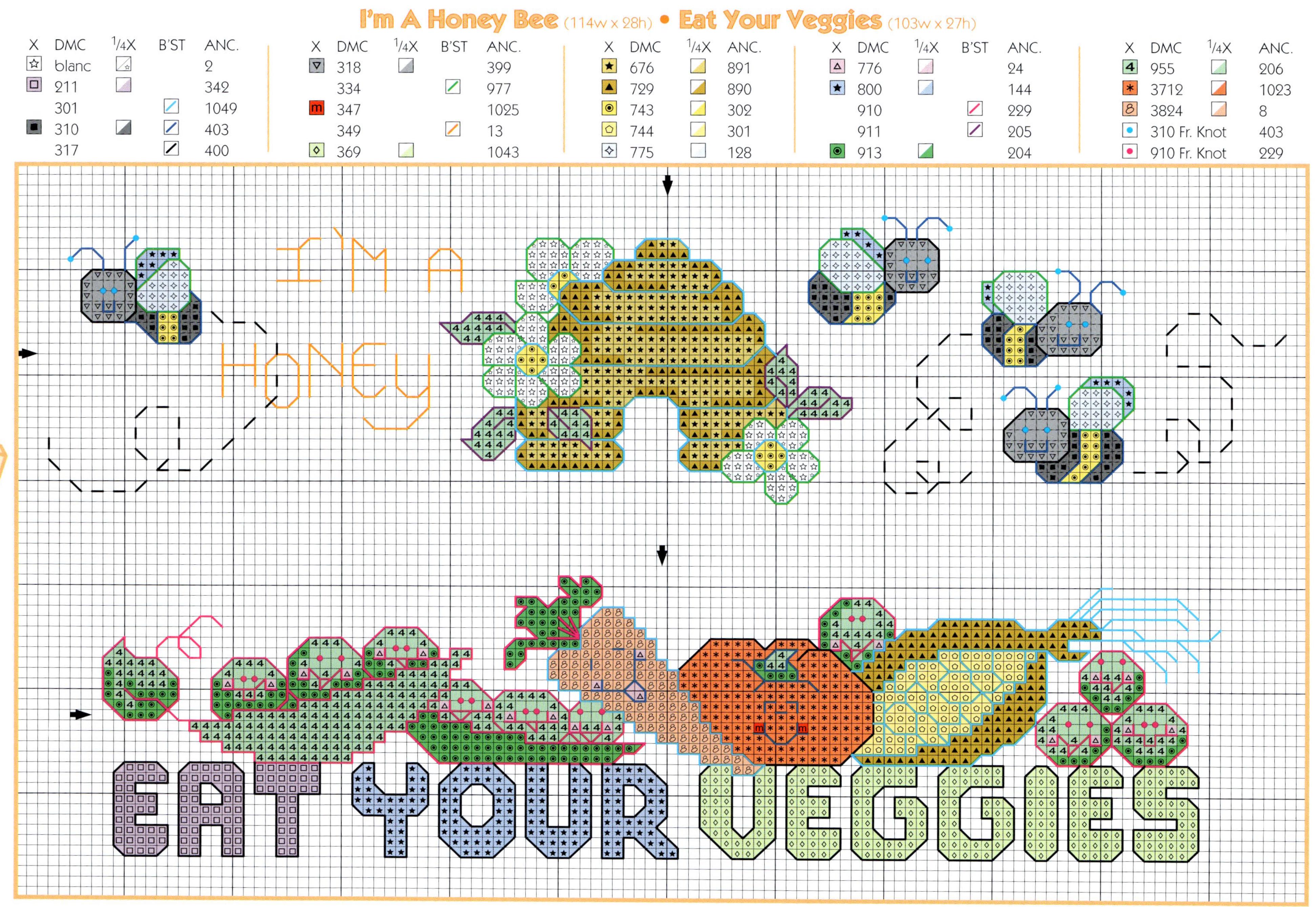

I'm A Honey Bee (114w x 28h) • Eat Your Veggies (103w x 27h)

X DMC ¼X B'ST ANC.
blanc 2
211 342
301 1049
310 403
317 400

X DMC ¼X B'ST ANC.
318 399
334 977
347 1025
349 13
369 1043

X DMC ¼X ANC.
676 891
729 890
743 302
744 301
775 128

X DMC ¼X B'ST ANC.
776 24
800 144
910 229
911 205
913 204

X DMC ¼X ANC.
955 206
3712 1023
3824 8
310 Fr. Knot 403
910 Fr. Knot 229

I'M A
HONEY
EAT YOUR VEGGIES
15

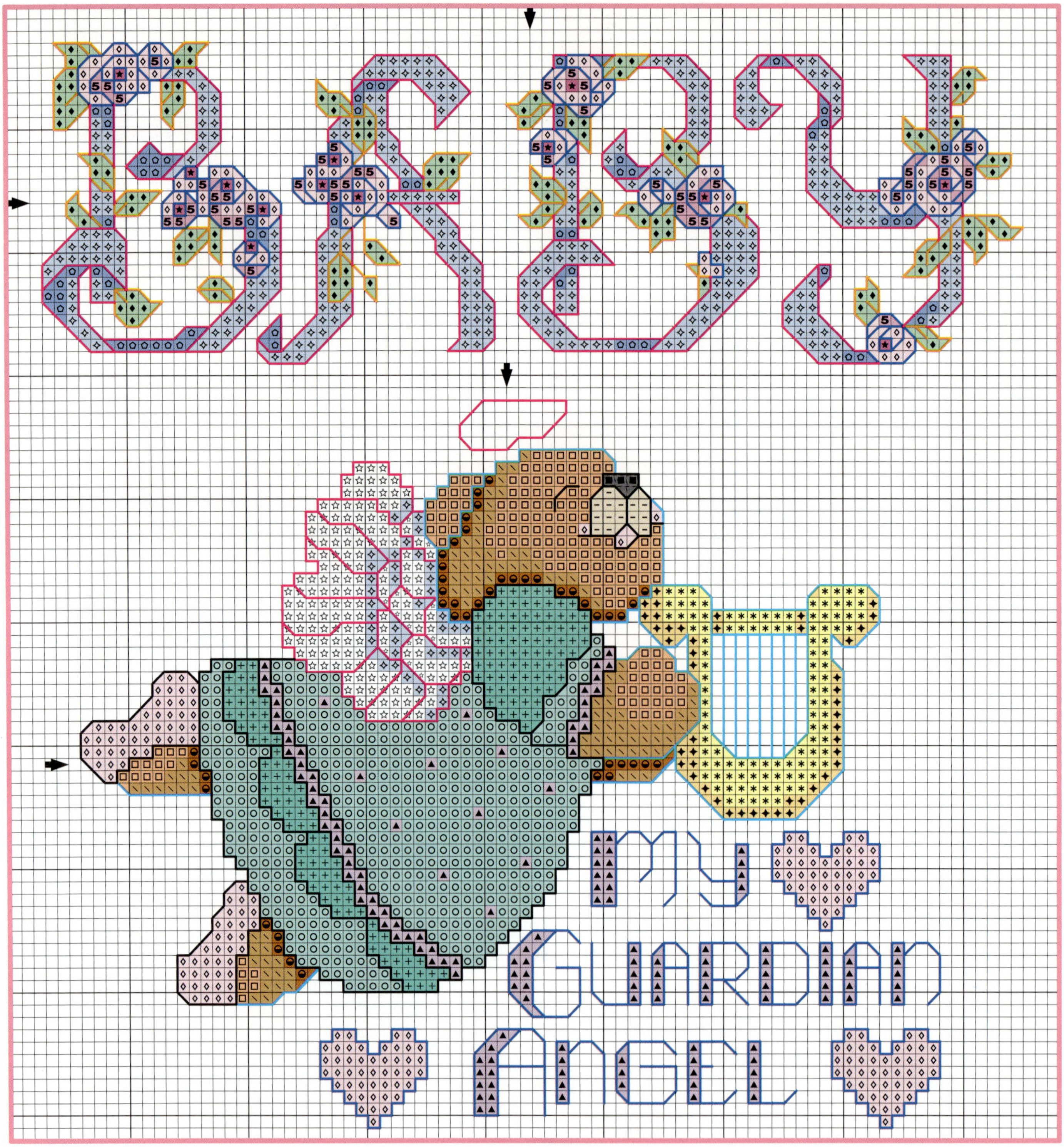

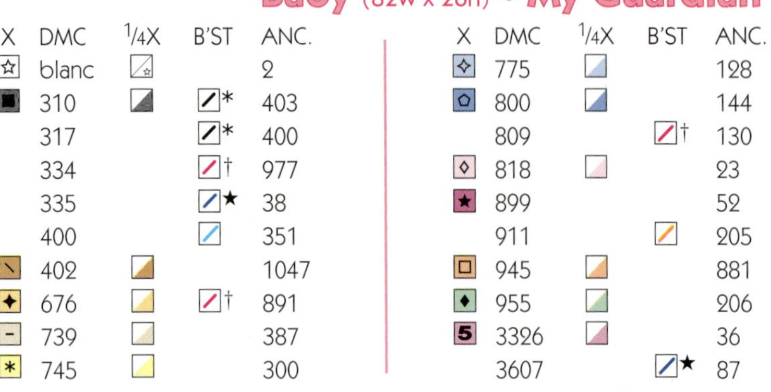

Baby (82w x 26h) • My Guardian Angel (72w x 59h)

X	DMC	1/4X	B'ST	ANC.
☆	blanc			2
■	310		✓*	403
	317		✓*	400
	334		✓†	977
	335		✓★	38
	400		✓	351
\	402			1047
◆	676		✓†	891
−	739			387
*	745			300

X	DMC	1/4X	B'ST	ANC.
◈	775			128
⬠	800			144
	809		✓†	130
◇	818			23
★	899			52
	911		✓	205
▢	945			881
◆	955			206
5	3326			36
	3607		✓★	87

X	DMC	1/4X	ANC.
▲	3609		85
+	3766		167
⬤	3776		1048
○	3811		1060

* DMC 310 for facial features. DMC 317 for dress and slippers.

† DMC 334 for letters. DMC 676 for halo. DMC 809 for wings.

★ DMC 335 for flowers. DMC 3607 for wording and hearts.

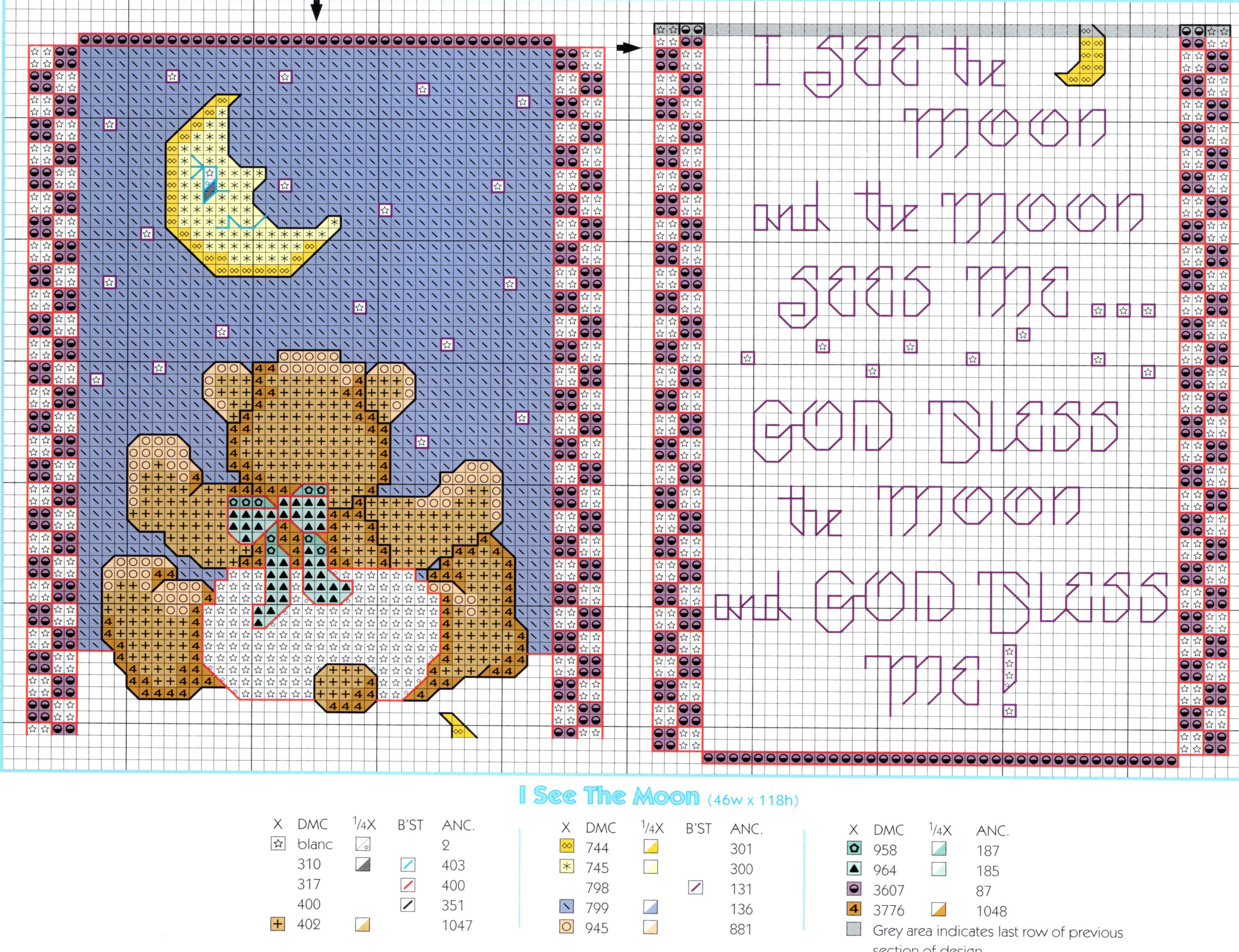

I See The Moon (46w x 118h)

X	DMC	1/4X	B'ST	ANC.
☆	blanc			2
	310		(blue)	403
	317		(red)	400
	400		(black)	351
+	402			1047

X	DMC	1/4X	B'ST	ANC.
⊗	744			301
✳	745			300
	798			131
	799			136
○	945			881

X	DMC	1/4X	ANC.
	958		187
▲	964		185
	3607		87
4	3776		1048

Grey area indicates last row of previous section of design.

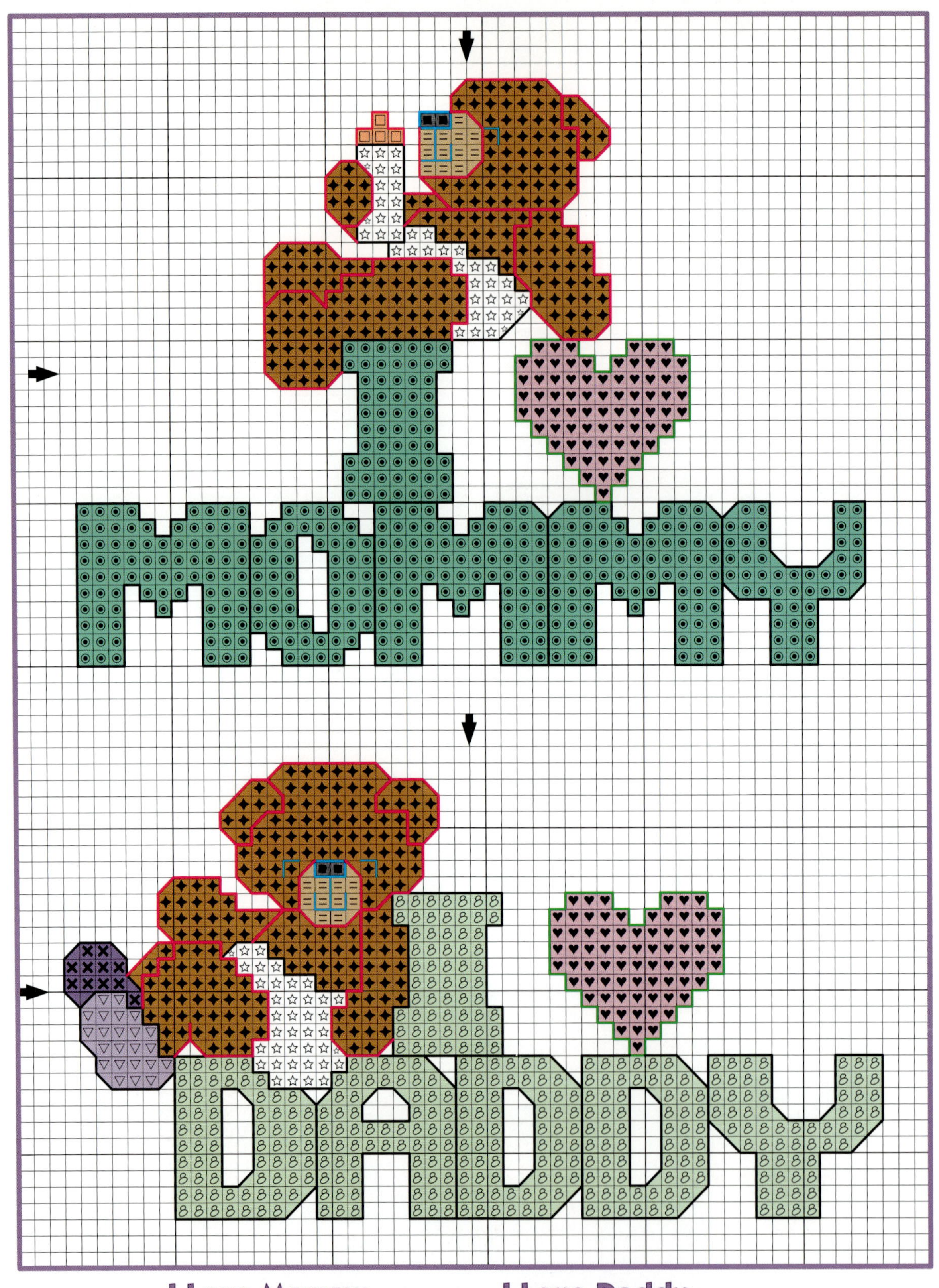

I Love Mommy (50w x 36h) • I Love Daddy (52w x 28h)

X	DMC	1/4X	B'ST	ANC.
☆	blanc			2
✖	209			109
▽	211			342
	301			1049
■	310			403

X	DMC	1/4X	B'ST	ANC.
	317			400
	335			38
◻	353			6
◆	738			361
=	739			387

X	DMC	1/4X	ANC.
♥	776		24
8	954		203
◉	959		186

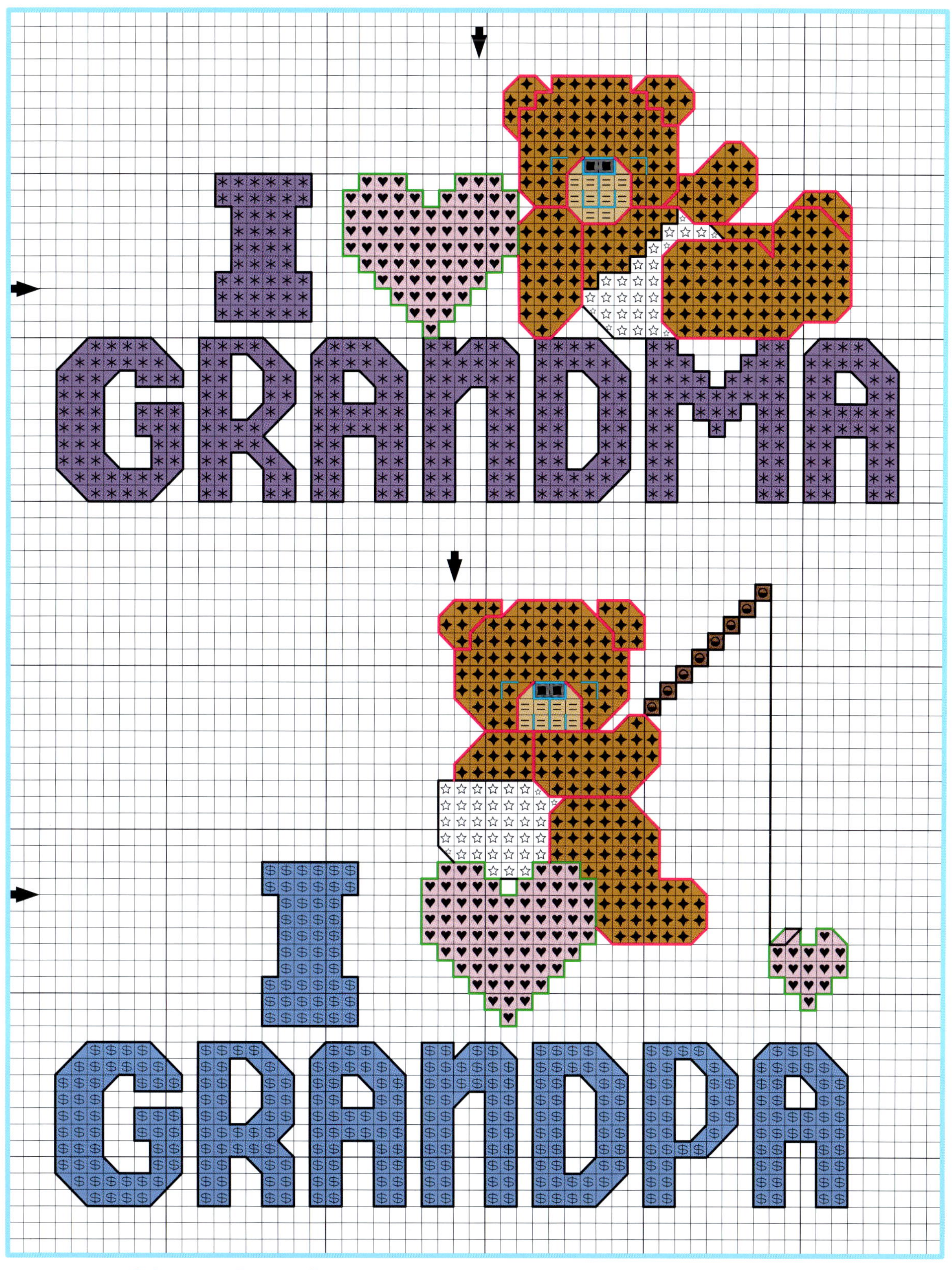

I Love Grandma (53w x 26h) • I Love Grandpa (50w x 38h)

X	DMC	1/4X	B'ST	ANC.		X	DMC	1/4X	ANC.
☆	blanc			2		●	437		362
✳	210			108		✦	738		361
	301			1049		=	739		387
■	310			403		♥	776		24
	317			400		$	800		144
	335			38					

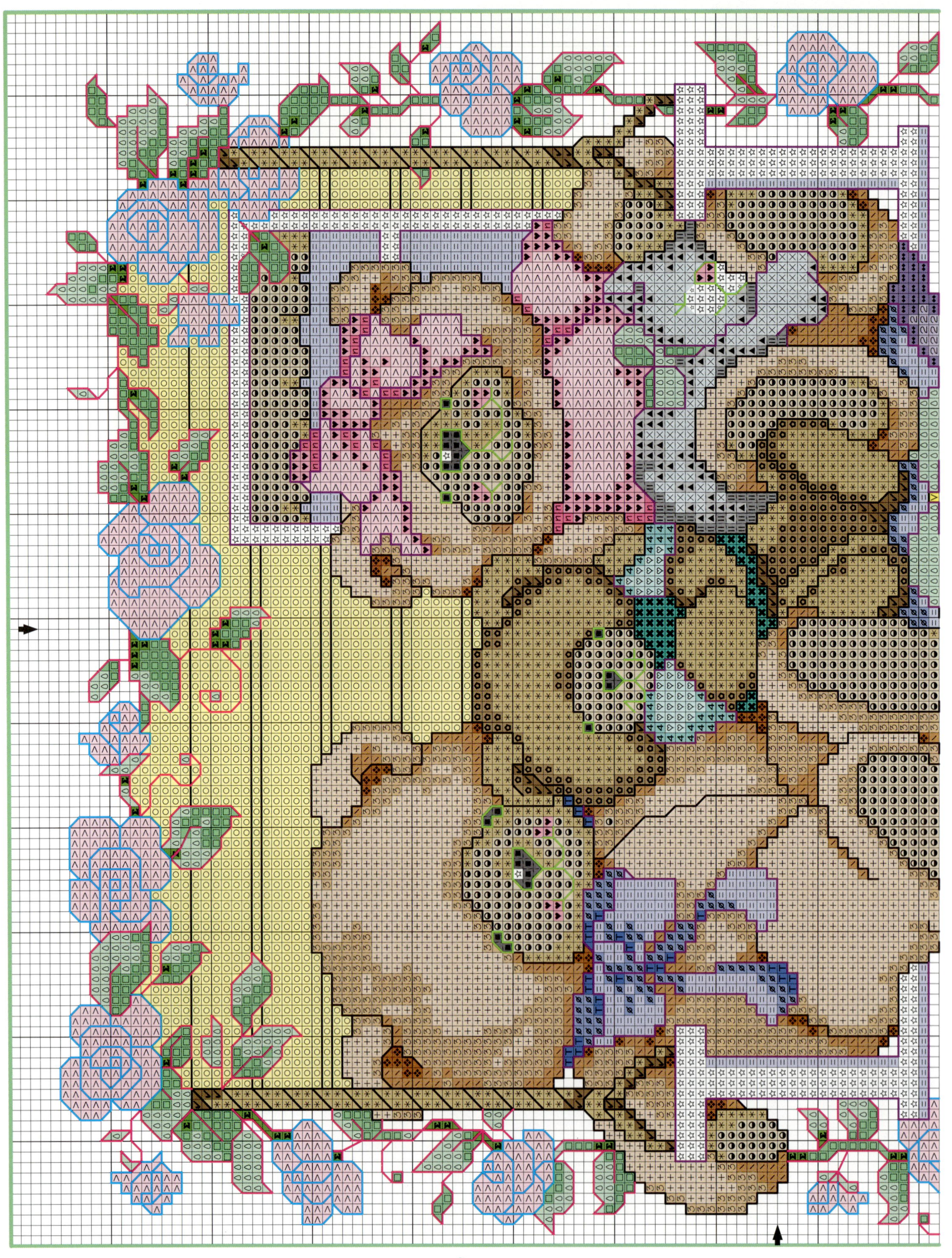

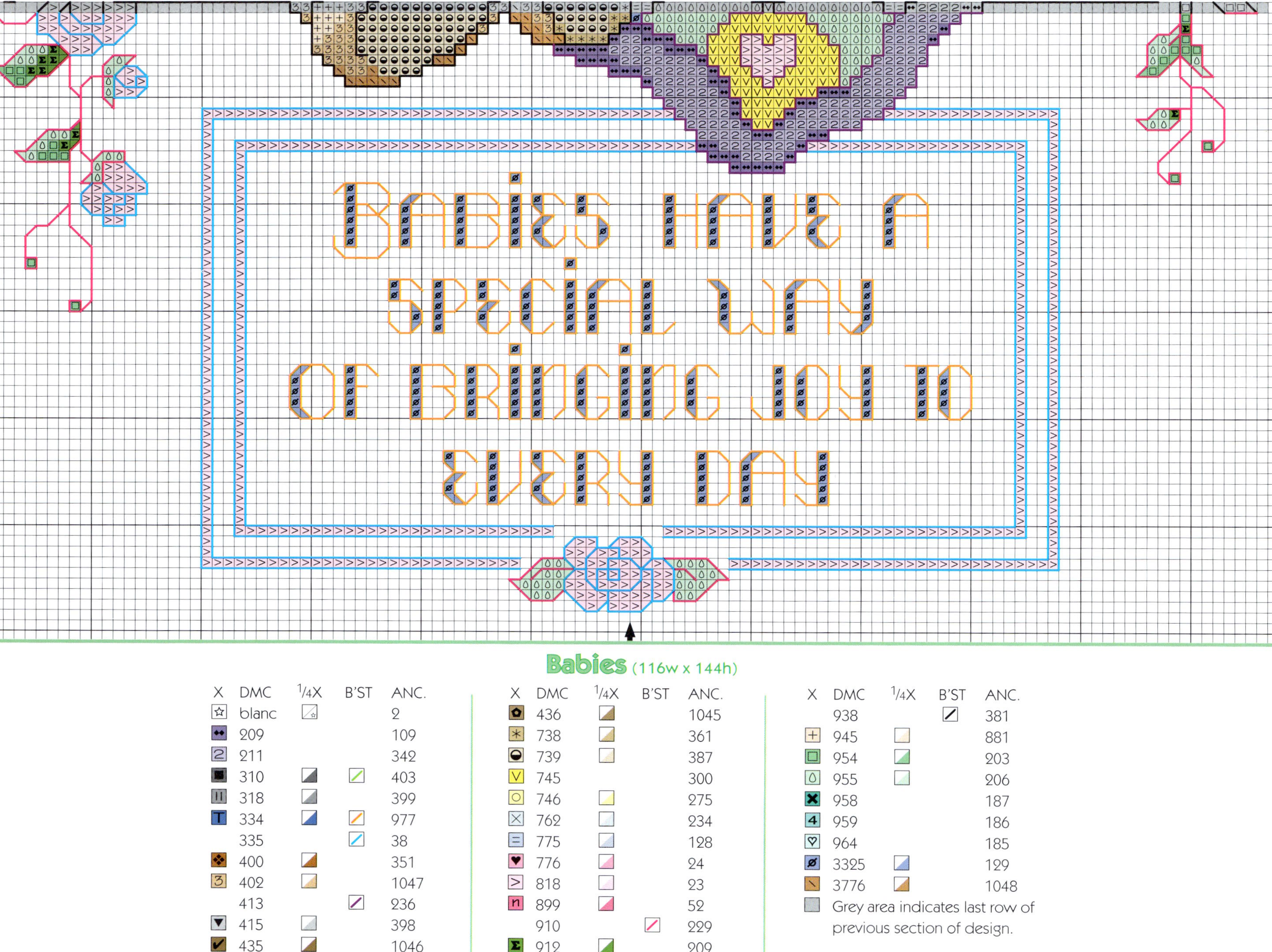

Babies (116w x 144h)

X	DMC	1/4X	B'ST	ANC.
☆	blanc			2
	209			109
	211			342
	310			403
	318			399
	334			977
	335			38
	400			351
	402			1047
	413			236
	415			398
	435			1046

X	DMC	1/4X	B'ST	ANC.
	436			1045
	738			361
	739			387
	745			300
	746			275
	762			234
	775			128
	776			24
	818			23
	899			52
	910			229
	912			209

X	DMC	1/4X	B'ST	ANC.
	938			381
	945			881
	954			203
	955			206
	958			187
	959			186
	964			185
	3325			129
	3776			1048

Grey area indicates last row of previous section of design.

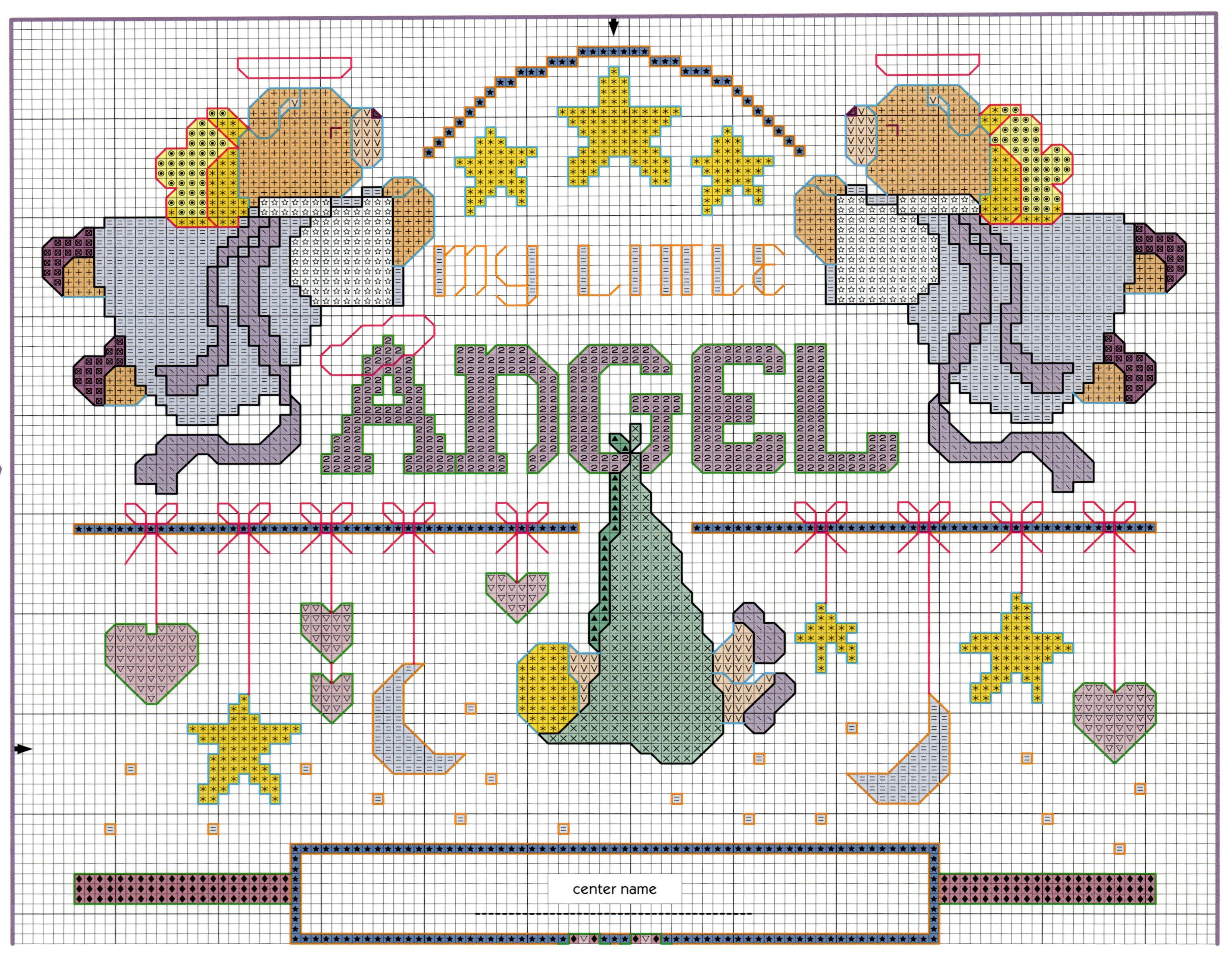

my LITTLE
ANGEL
center name

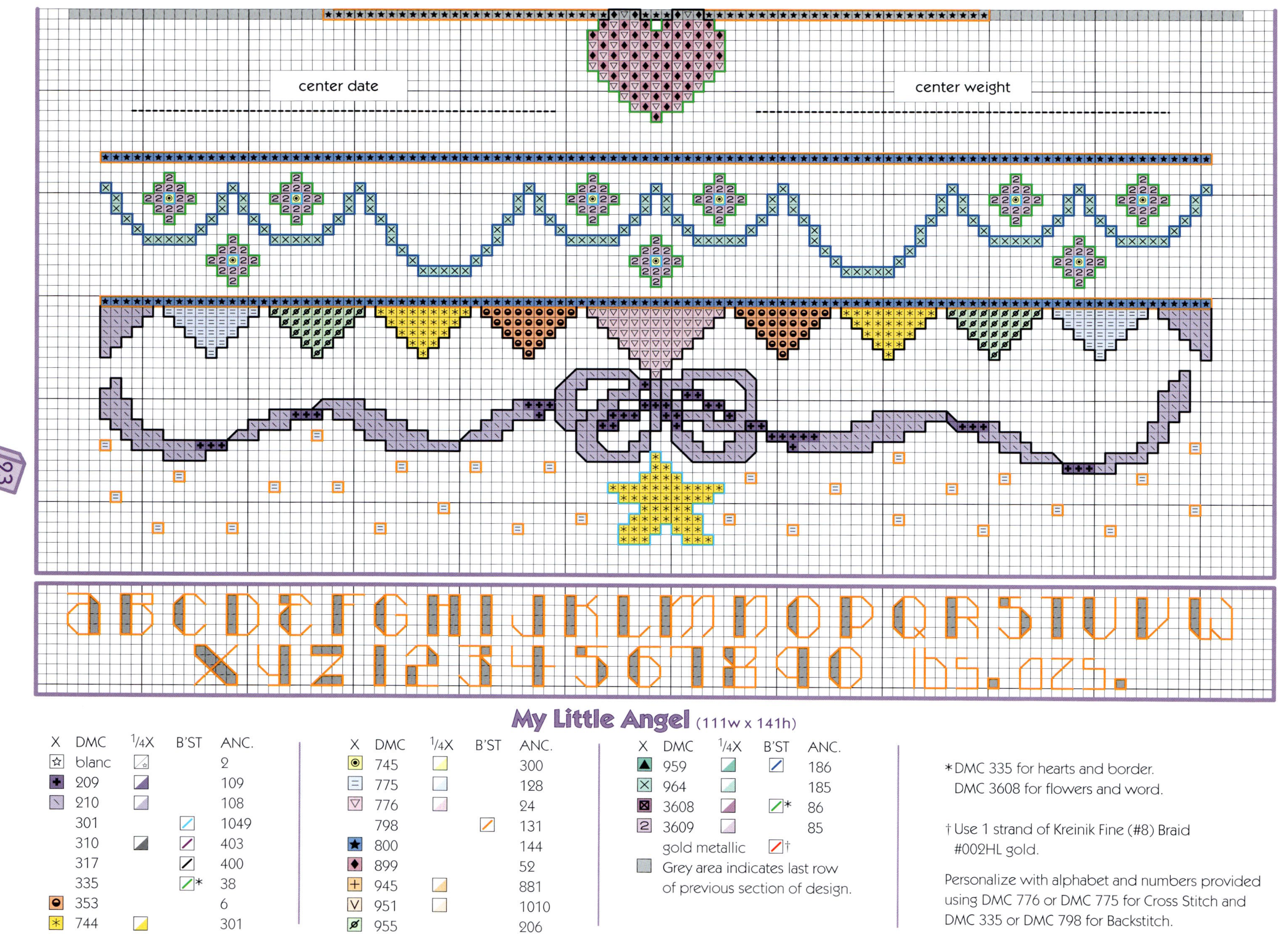

My Little Angel (111w x 141h)

X	DMC	1/4X	B'ST	ANC.
☆	blanc			2
✚	209			109
	210			108
	301		(1/4X)	1049
	310		(1/4X)	403
	317		(1/4X)	400
	335		(1/4X)*	38
◉	353			6
✳	744			301

X	DMC	1/4X	B'ST	ANC.
◉	745			300
=	775			128
▽	776			24
	798		(B'ST)	131
★	800			144
◆	899			52
+	945			881
V	951			1010
ø	955			206

X	DMC	1/4X	B'ST	ANC.
◣	959			186
✕	964			185
⊠	3608		*	86
2	3609			85
	gold metallic		†	
	Grey area indicates last row of previous section of design.			

*DMC 335 for hearts and border. DMC 3608 for flowers and word.

† Use 1 strand of Kreinik Fine (#8) Braid #002HL gold.

Personalize with alphabet and numbers provided using DMC 776 or DMC 775 for Cross Stitch and DMC 335 or DMC 798 for Backstitch.

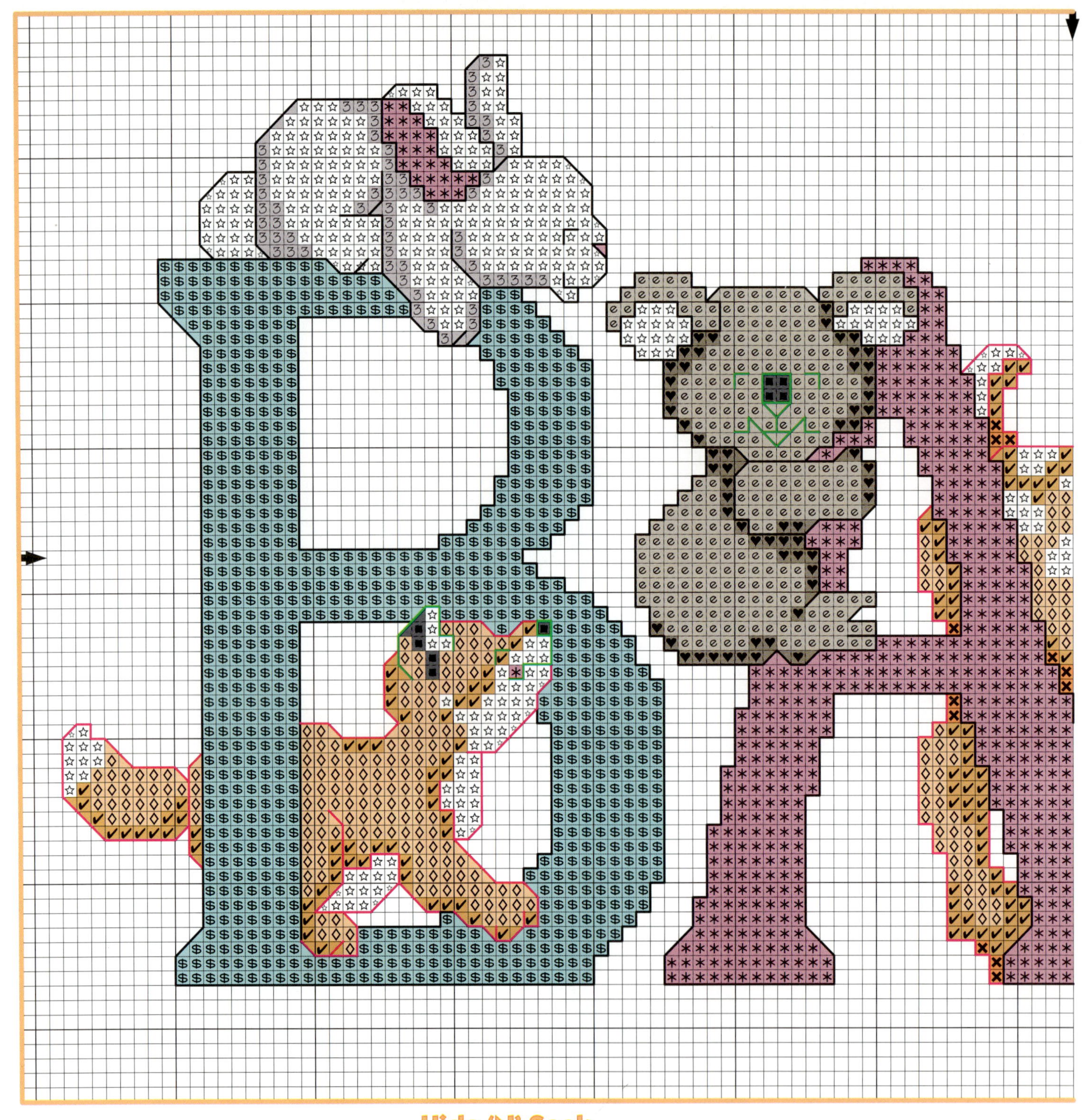

Hide 'N' Seek (144w x 69h)

X	DMC	1/4X	B'ST	ANC.		X	DMC	1/4X	ANC.		X	DMC	1/4X	ANC.
☆	blanc	☆		2		♥	642		392		◇	945		881
4	211			342		e	644		830		2	955		206
■	310		✓	403		m	738		361		✖	3776		1048
✚	400		✗	351		3	762		234		$	3811		1060
✓	402			1047		=	775		128		●	310 Fr. Knot		403
◢	413		✓	236		✳	776		24			Grey area indicates last row		
⊙	437			362		◎	800		144			of previous section of design.		

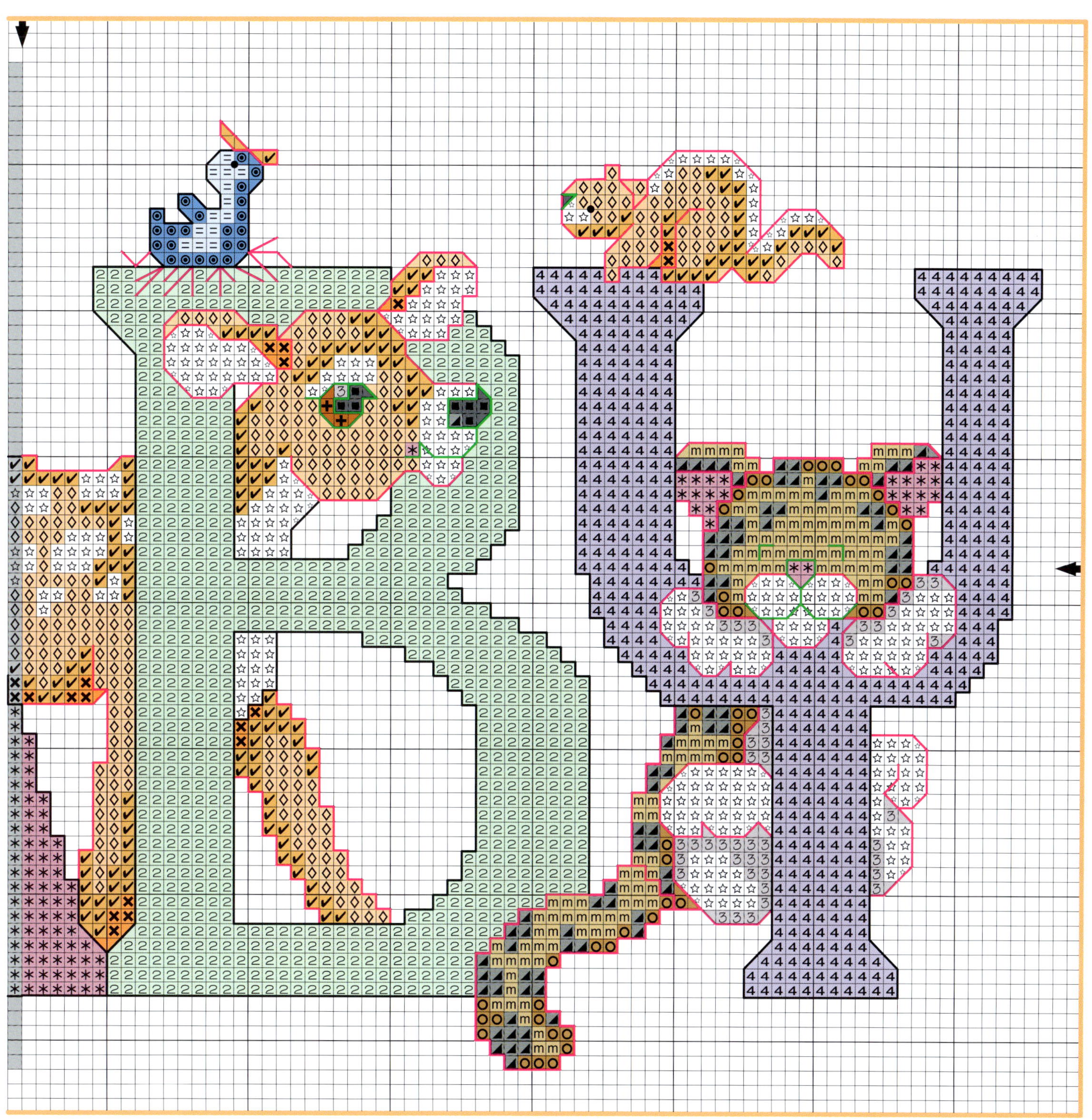

Help Us, Father

(112w x 86h)

X	DMC	¼X	B'ST	ANC.
☆	blanc			2
◆	209		╱	109
⬠	350		╱*	11
	367		╱	217
⊗	368			214
◆	402			1047
★	435			1046
○	437			362
✕	676			891
♡	722			323
=	739			387
Π	776			24
▢	800			144
	839		╱	1086
◆	840			1084
╲	945			881
P	958			187
✔	959			186
	975		╱*	355
⊙	3755			140
⊖	3776			1048
✳	3782			899
■	3799		╱	236
▲	3814		╱	1074
●	3799 Fr. Knot			236

Grey area indicates last row of
previous section of design.

*DMC 350 for kite tail. DMC 975
for all other.

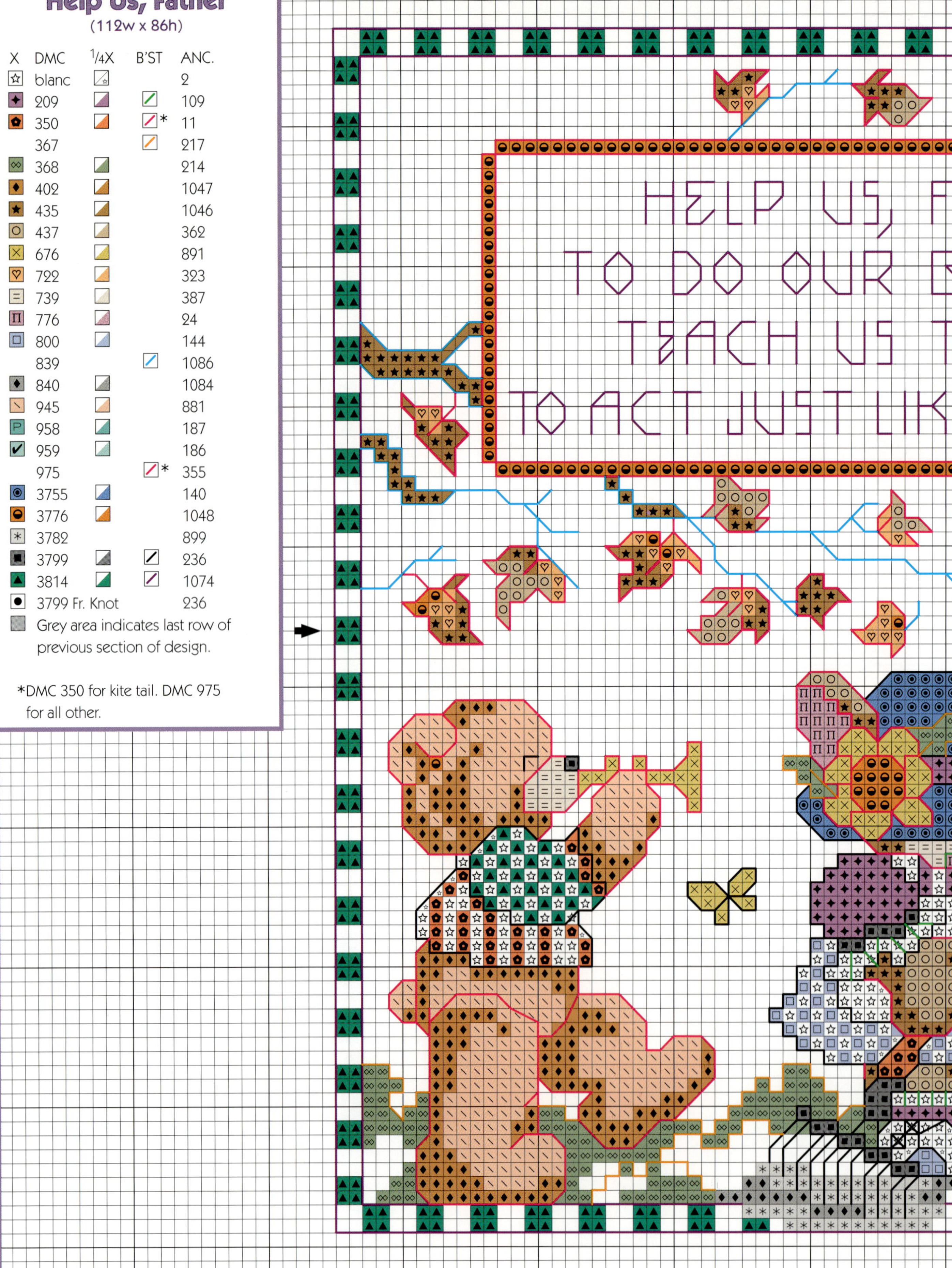

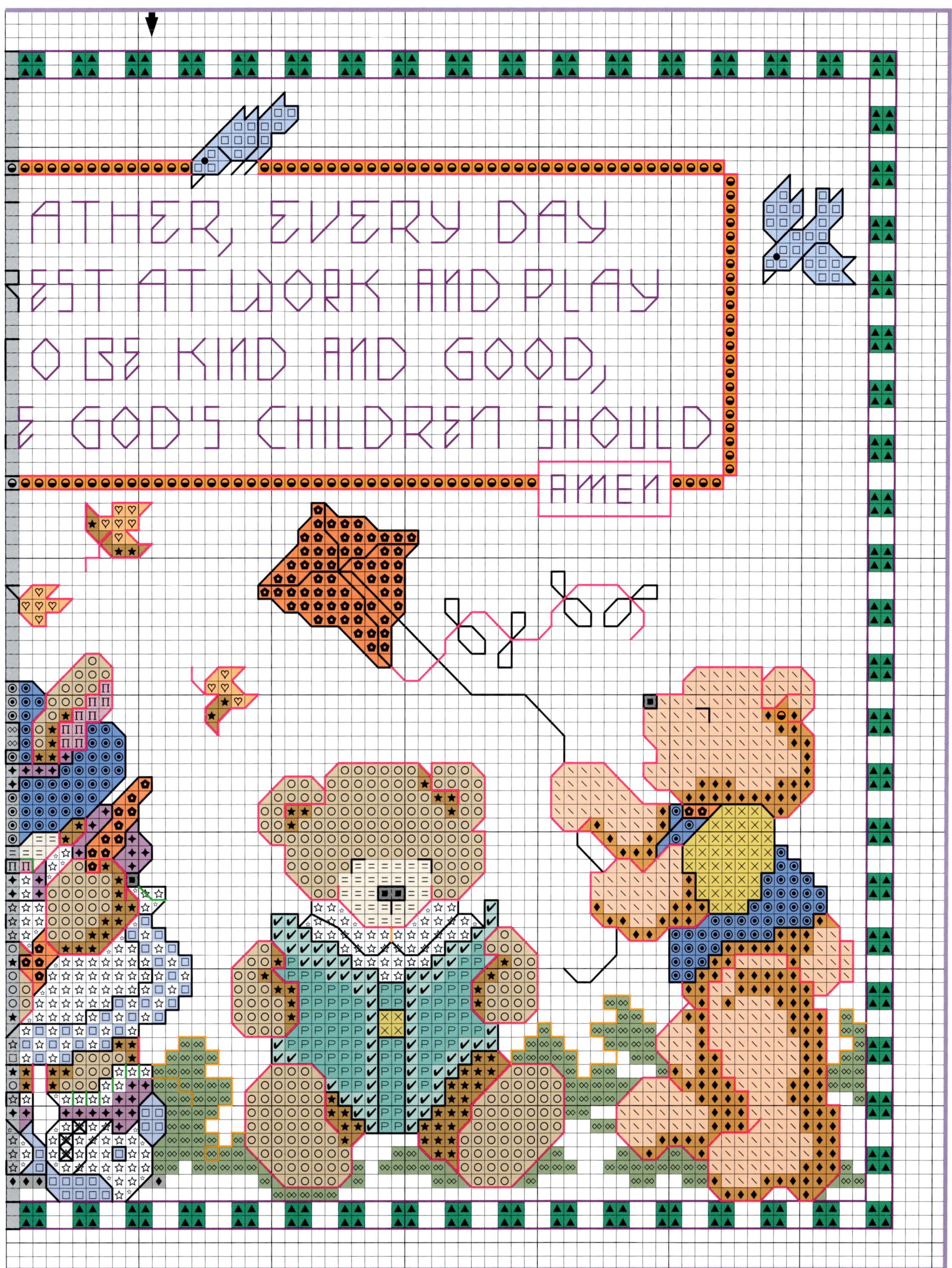
ATHER, EVERY DAY
EST AT WORK AND PLAY
O BE KIND AND GOOD,
S GOD'S CHILDREN SHOULD
AMEN

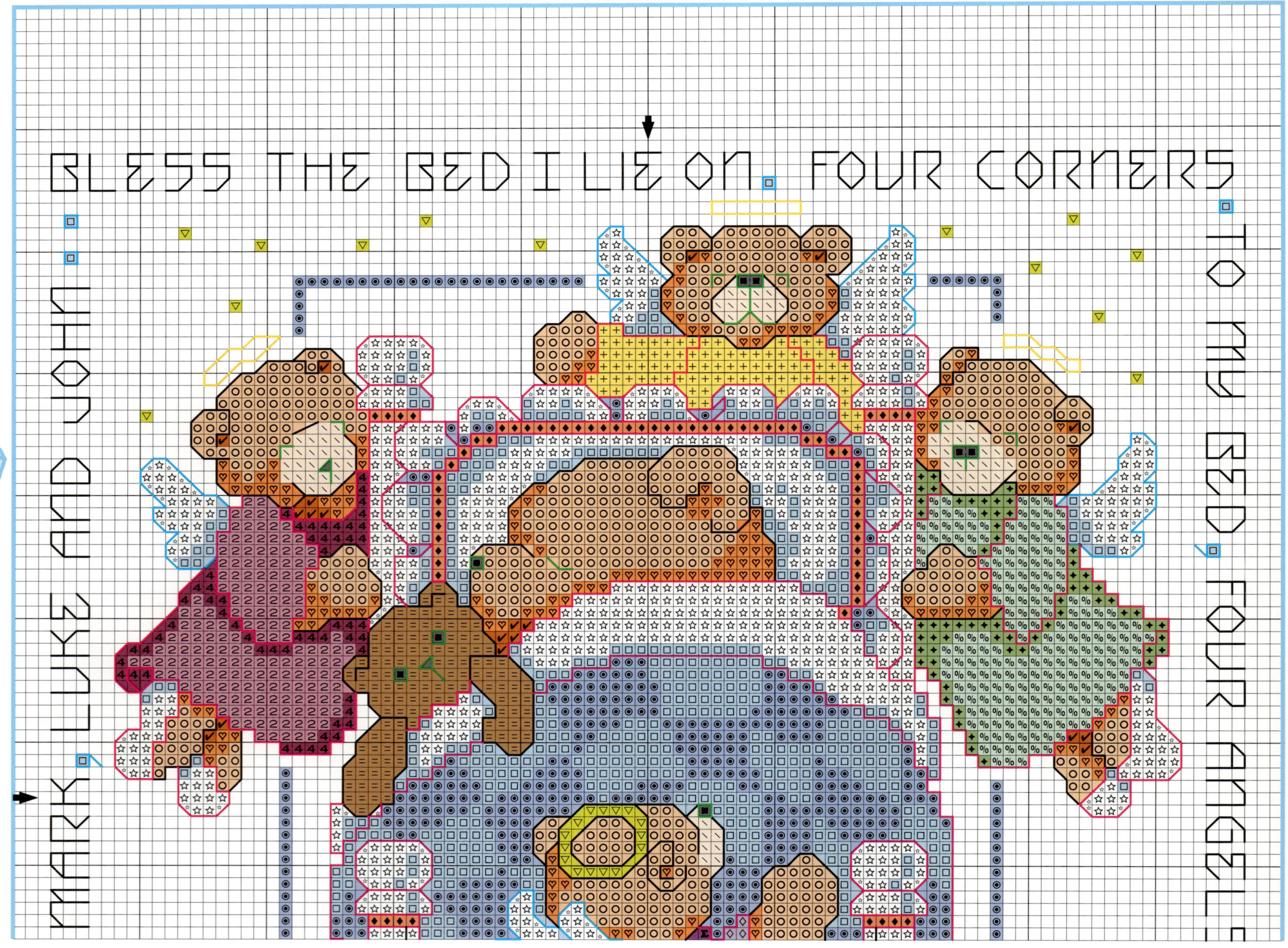

BLESS THE BED I LIE ON, FOUR CORNERS
TO MY BED, FOUR ANGELS
MARK LUKE AND JOHN

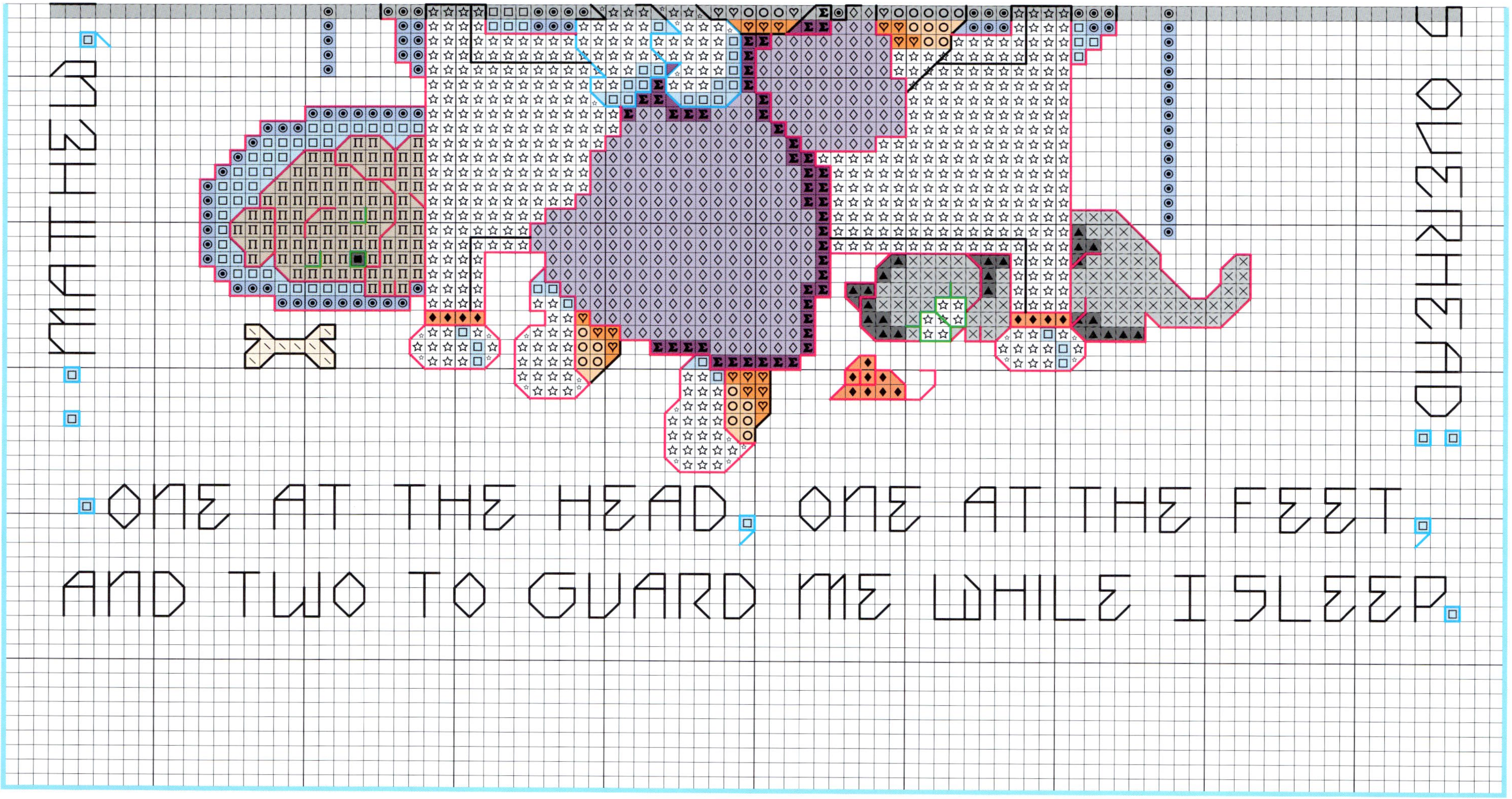

Matthew, Mark, Luke, And John (94w x 105h)

X	DMC	1/4X	B'ST	ANC.
☆	blanc	◩		2
◇	211	◩		342
	309		/*	42
	317		/	400
▲	318	◩		399
	349		/*	13
◆	350	◩		11
♡	402	◩		1047
☒	415	◩		398

X	DMC	1/4X	B'ST	ANC.
Σ	554	◩		96
✦	563	◩		208
=	738	◩		361
+	745	◩		300
◉	800	◩		144
Π	842	◩		1080
✔	922	◩		1003
	931		/	1034
○	945	◩		881

X	DMC	1/4X	B'ST	ANC.
%	955	◩		206
2	963	◩		73
	975		/*	355
4	3354	◩		74
□	3756	◩		1037
⟍	3774	◩		778
■	3799	◩	/	236
▽†		◩	/	Kreinik Fine (#8) Braid #002 gold

Grey area indicates last row of previous section of design.

* DMC 309 for wording. DMC 349 for bed. DMC 975 for all other.

† Use **1** strand.

Two Little Eyes

(77w x 151h)

X	DMC	¼X	B'ST	ANC.
☆	blanc	☆		2
Π	210	Π		108
	322		✓ *	978
▲	334	▲		977
	335		✓	38
	350		✓ †	11
	434		✓ *	310
✓	437	✓		362
	553		✓	98
	561		✓	212
+	562			210
=	739	=		387
O	745			300
◉	800			144
▽	954	▽		203
◇	963	◇		73
%	3341	%		328
n	3354	n		74
□	3756	□		1037
■	3799		✓ †	236
	3799 & #001		✓ ★	236

☐ Grey area indicates last row of previous section.

* DMC 434 for rabbits and yellow hearts. DMC 322 for all other.

† DMC 350 for hearts, carrots, and wording. DMC 3799 for all other.

★ Use 1 strand of floss and 1 strand of Kreinik Fine (#8) Braid #001 silver.

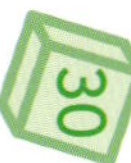

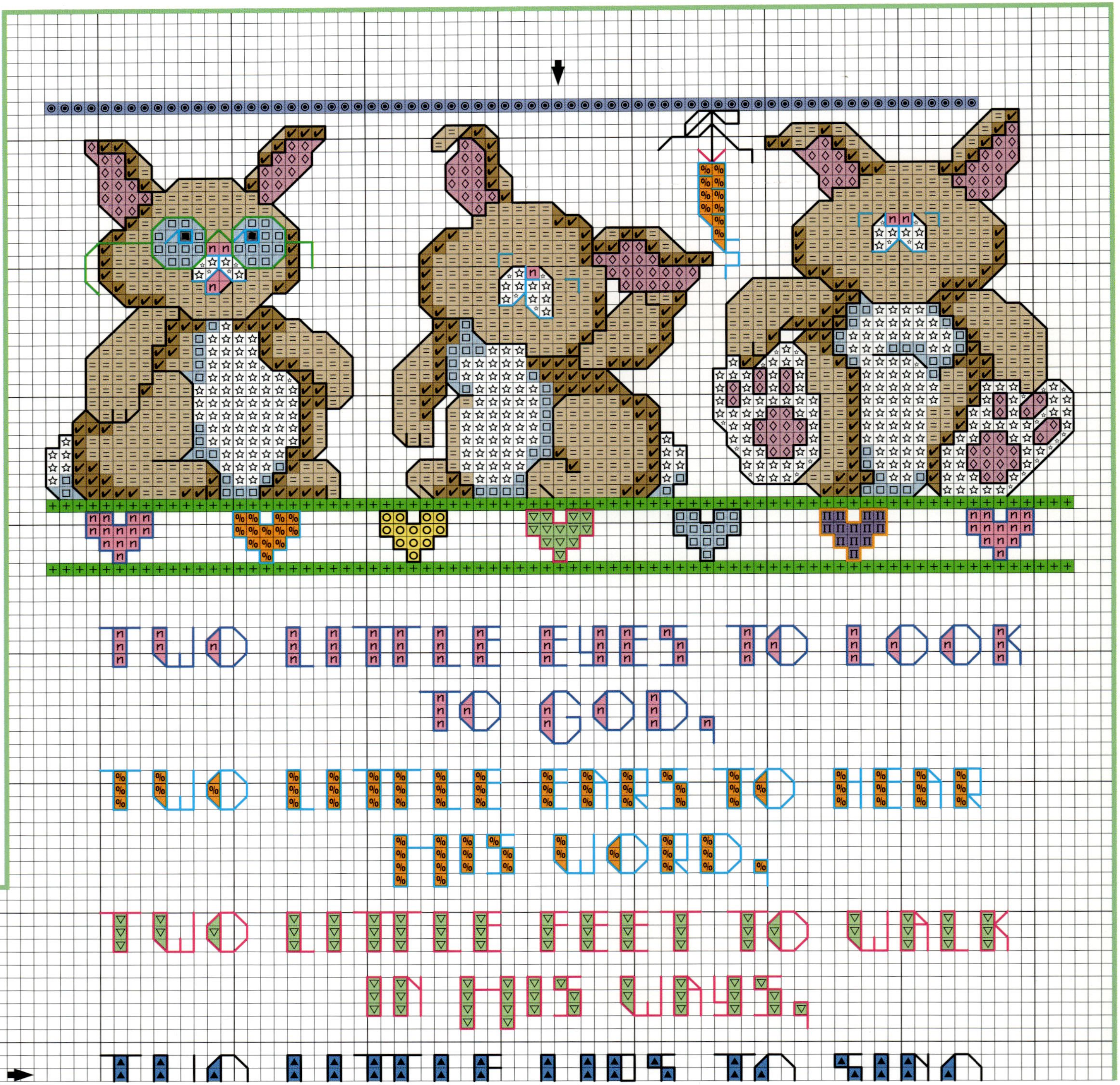

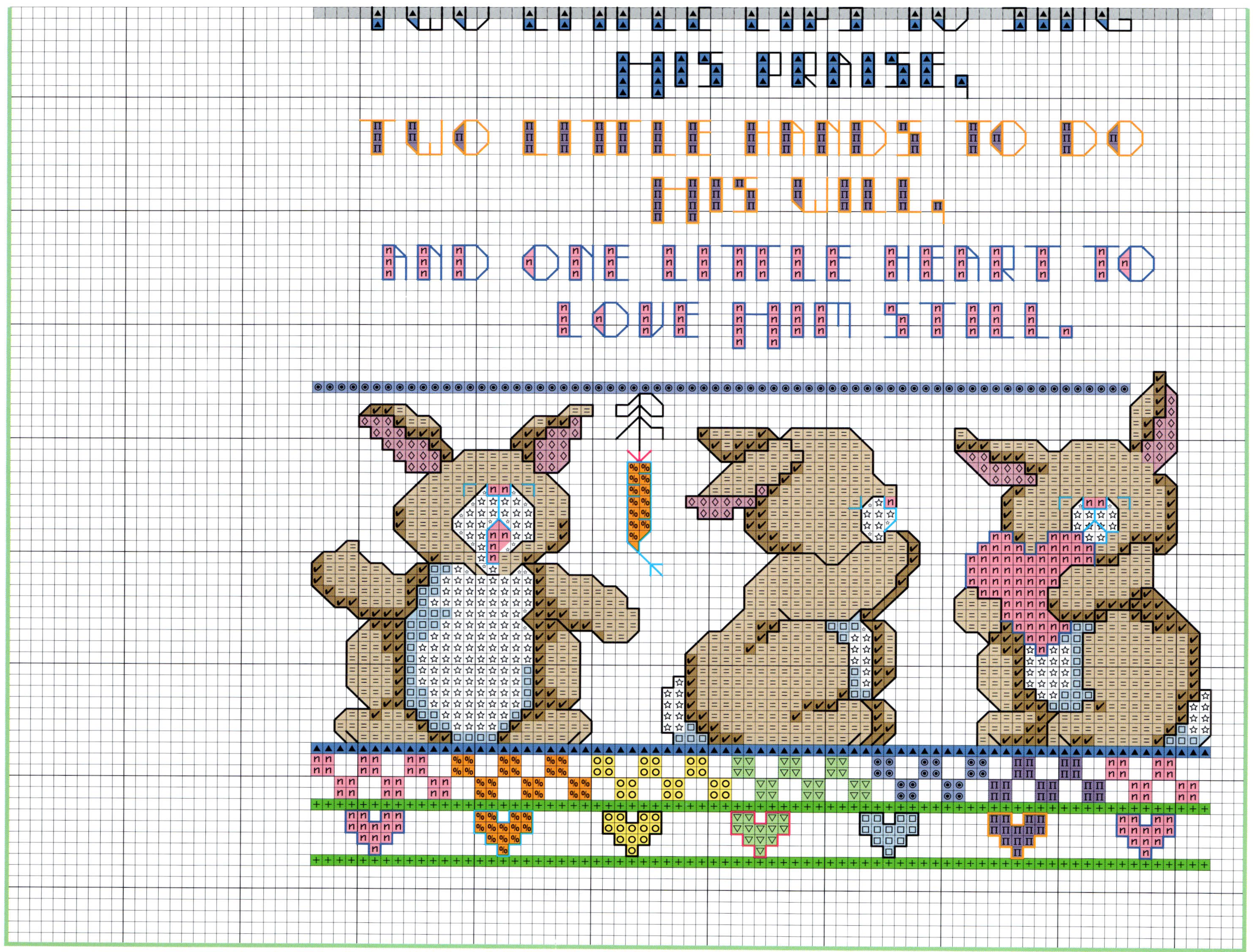

... LITTLE EYES ... TO SING
HIS PRAISE,
TWO LITTLE HANDS TO DO
HIS WILL,
AND ONE LITTLE HEART TO
LOVE HIM STILL.

NOW I LAY ME DOWN TO REST,
ANGELS GUARD ME IN MY NEST.
HEAVEN Y FATHER CARE FOR ME

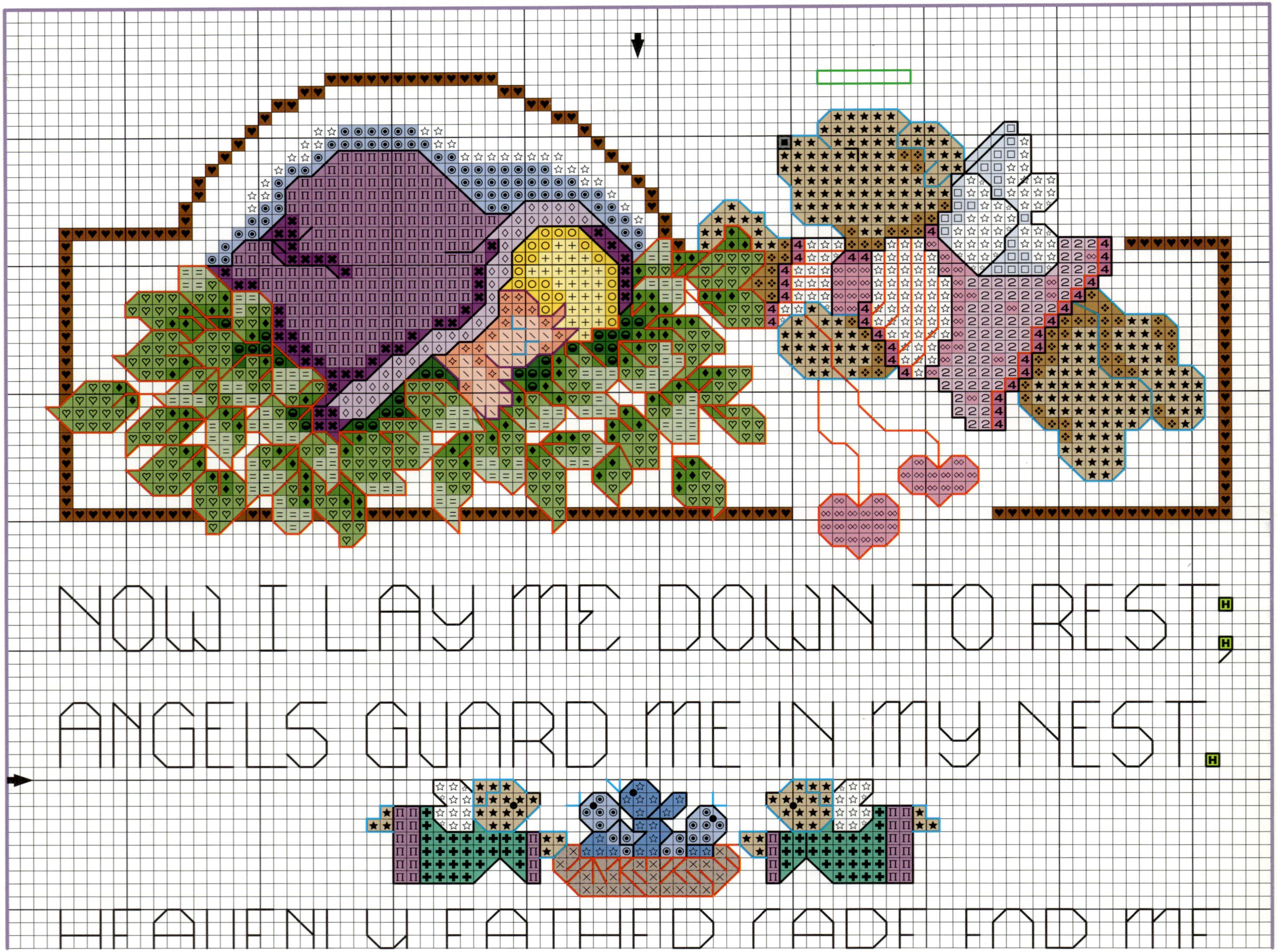

32

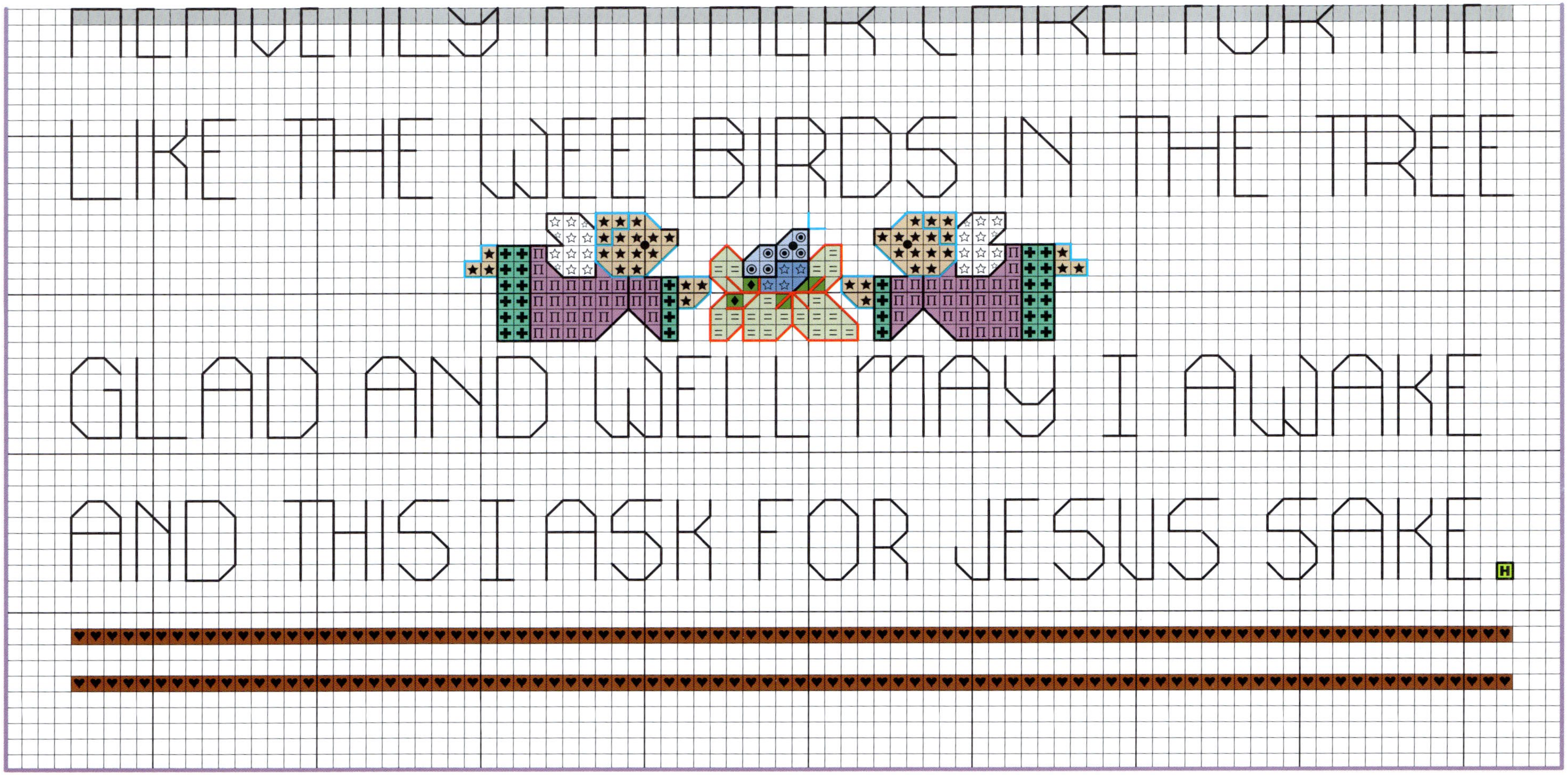

Now I Lay Me Down To Rest (89w x 110h)

X	DMC	1/4X	B'ST	ANC.	X	DMC	1/4X	B'ST	ANC.	X	DMC	1/4X	B'ST	ANC.	X	B'ST	
☆	blanc			2	+	745			300	♥	975			355			Kreinik Fine (#8)
✖	209			109		754			1012	⊟	987		†	244			Braid #002 gold
Π	210			108	✧	758			868	◆	3347			266			Grey area indicates last row of previous section of design.
◇	211			342	=	772			259	♡	3348			264			
	334		*	977	◉	775			128		3354			74			
	335		†	38	☆	800			144	4	3733			75			
	356			5975		839		†	1086	☐	3756			1037			
❖	436			1045	H	958		*	187	✕	3782			899			
★	437			362	✚	959			186	■	3799		*	236			
O	744			301	2	963			73	●	3799 Fr. Knot			236			

* DMC 334 for birds and small bears' wings. DMC 958 for wording. DMC 3799 for all other.

† DMC 839 for nest. DMC 987 for leaves. DMC 335 for all other.

Noah's Ark

(104w x 106h)

X	DMC	¼X	B'ST	ANC.
☆	blanc	◹		2
♡	210	◺		108
	300		╱	352
■	310	◺	╱	403
	312		╱	979
	335		╱	38
Σ	352	◺		9
▽	353	◺		6
✔	402	◺		1047
>	413	◺	╱	236
	561		╱	212
★	563	◺		208
%	738	◺		361
\	739	◺		387
O	743	◺		302
+	745	◺		300
◉	775	◺		128
✳	776	◺		24
‖	800	◺		144
	801		╱	359
❖	809	◺		130
◇	818			23
◆	899	◺		52
H	922	◺		1003
✧	955	◺		206
⊖	964	◺		185
✖	3032	◺		903
V	3033	◺		391
□	3756			1037
8	3782	◺		899
⬠	3790	◺		393
•	312 Fr. Knot			
•	561 Fr. Knot			

Grey area indicates first row of right section of design.

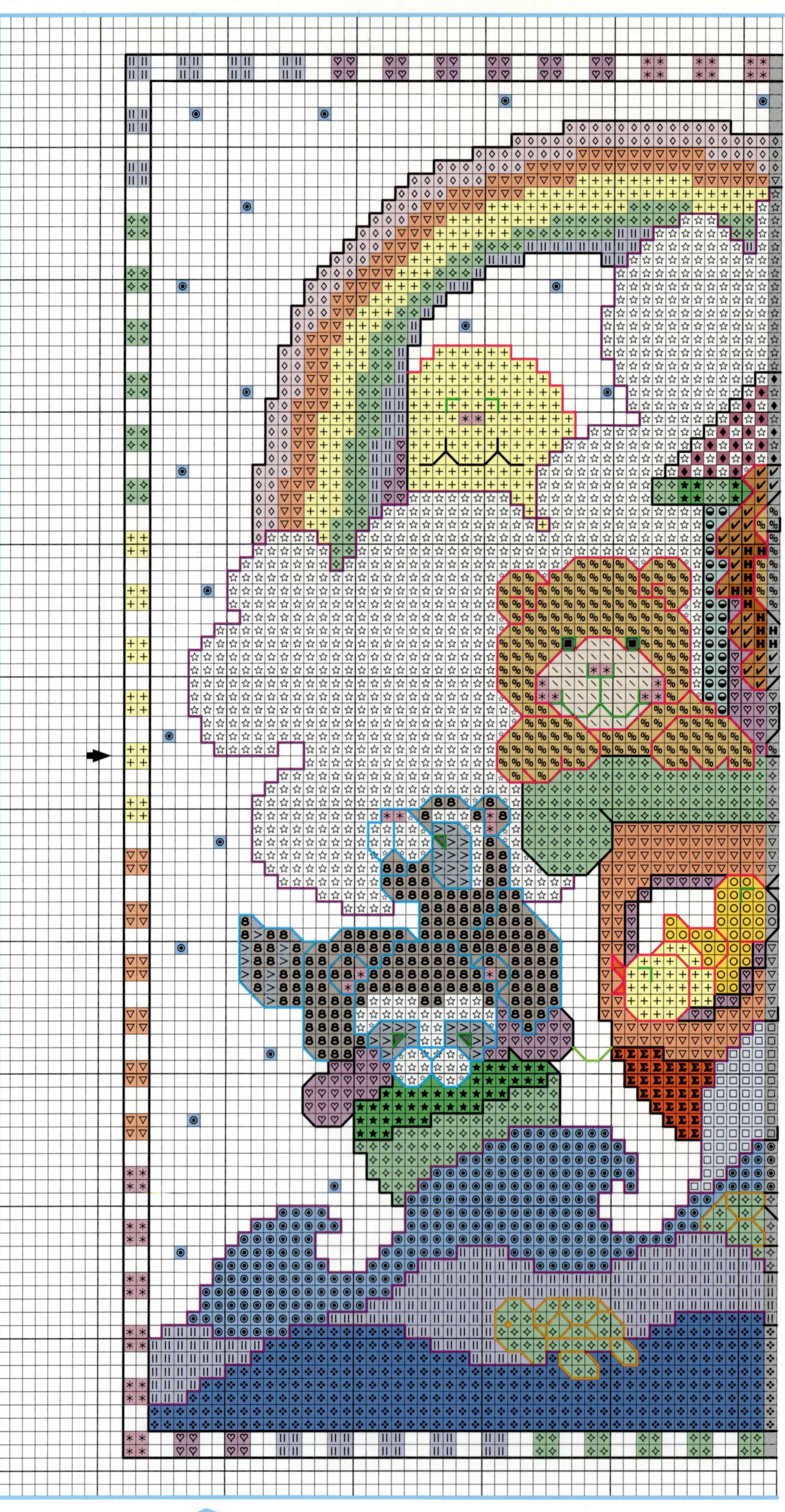

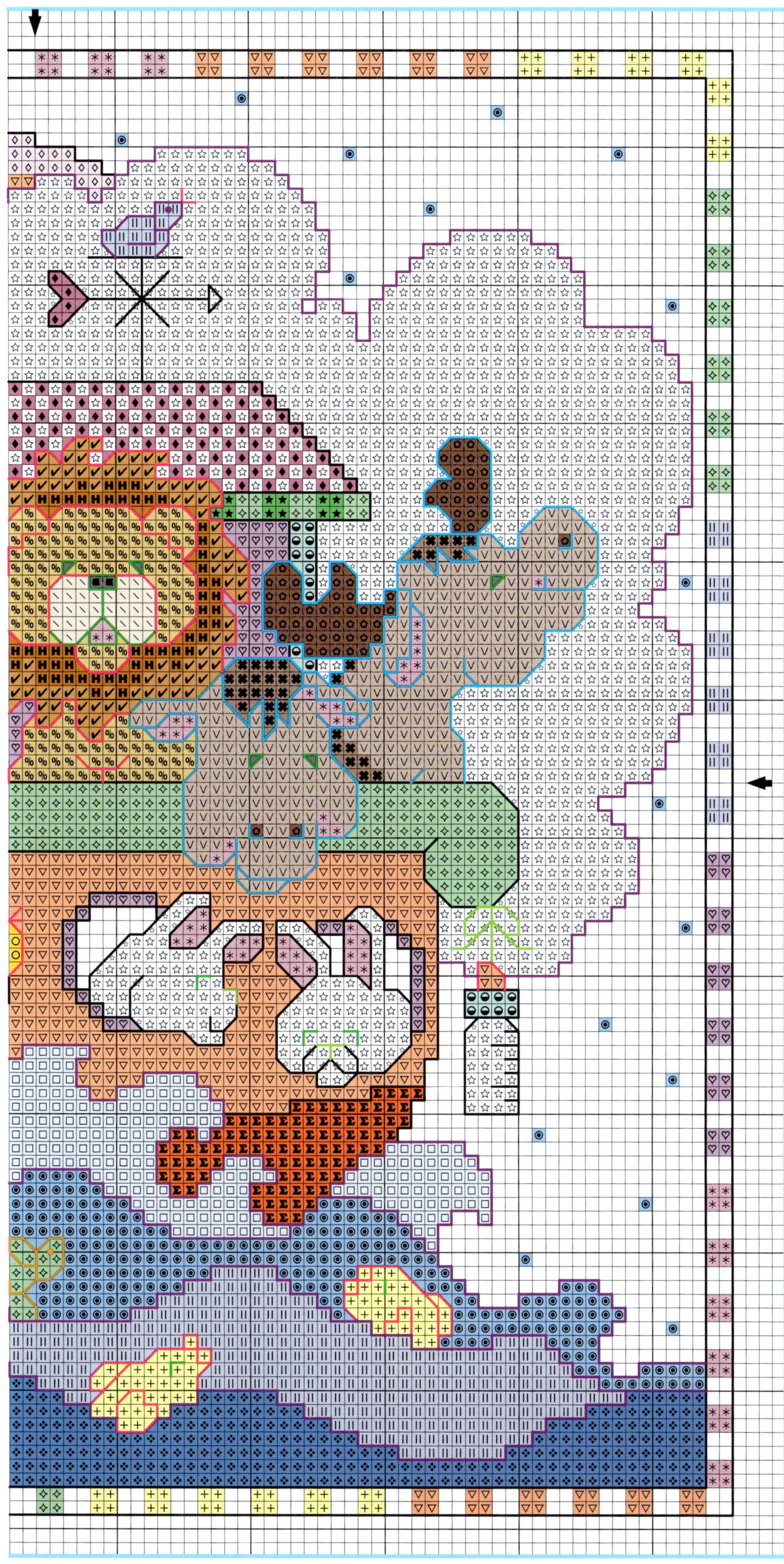

A Gift From God (120w x 188h)

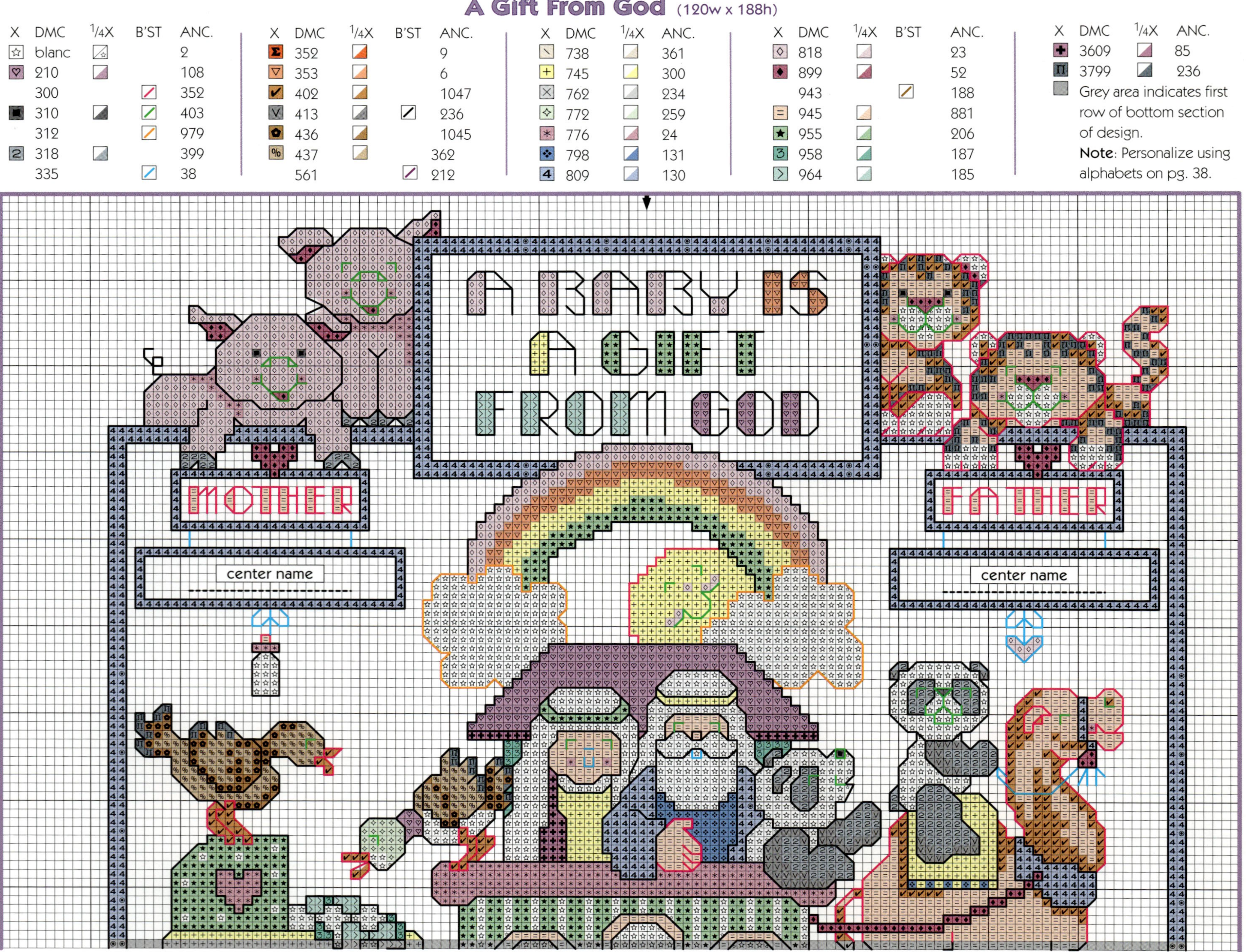

X	DMC	¼X	B'ST	ANC.
	blanc			2
	210			108
	300			352
	310			403
	312			979
	318			399
	335			38

X	DMC	¼X	B'ST	ANC.
	352			9
	353			6
	402			1047
	413			236
	436			1045
	437			362
	561			212

X	DMC	¼X	ANC.
	738		361
	745		300
	762		234
	772		259
	776		24
	798		131
	809		130

X	DMC	¼X	B'ST	ANC.
	818			23
	899			52
	943			188
	945			881
	955			206
	958			187
	964			185

X	DMC	¼X	ANC.
	3609		85
	3799		236

Grey area indicates first row of bottom section of design.

Note: Personalize using alphabets on pg. 38.

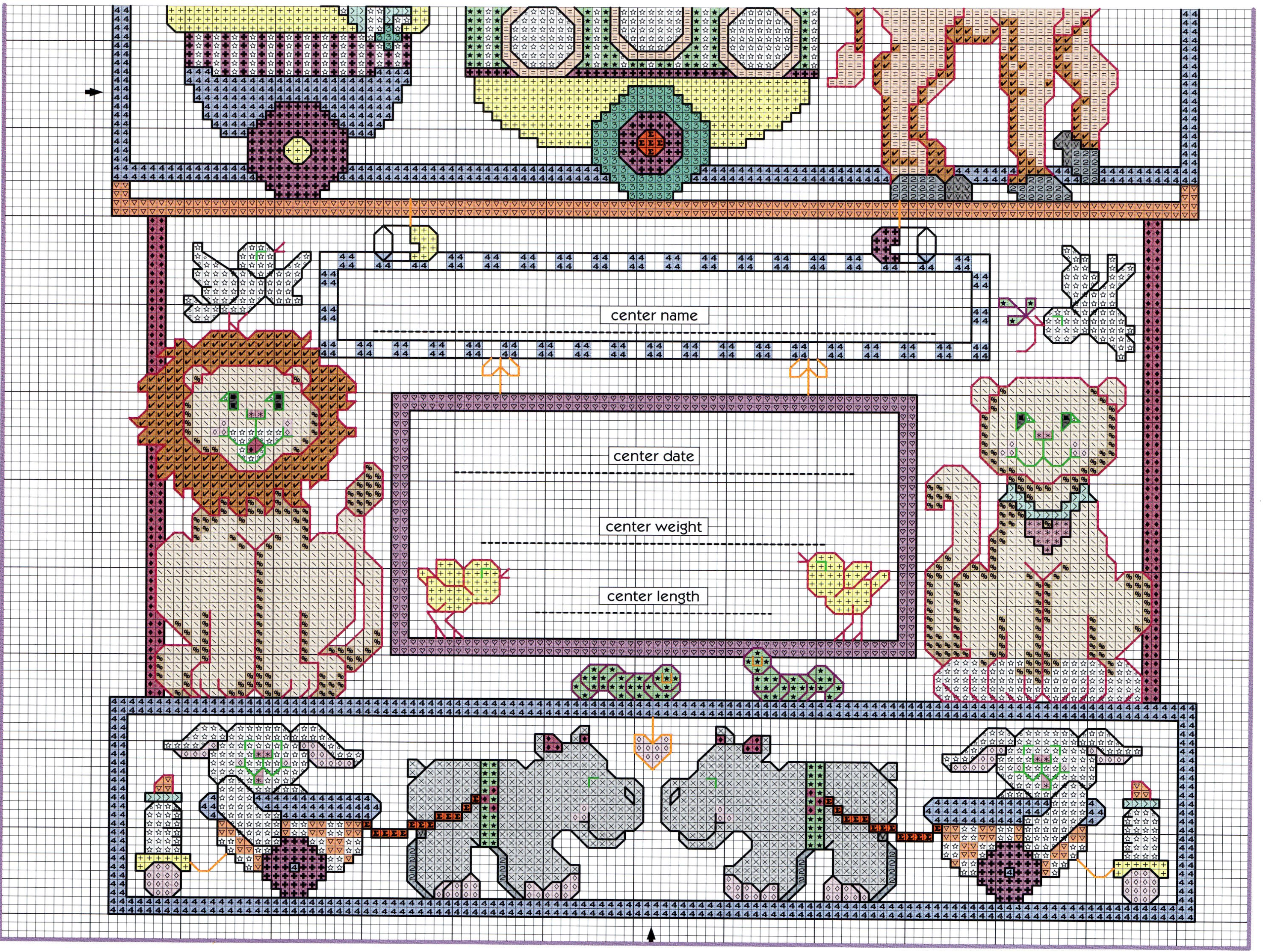

center name
center date
center weight
center length

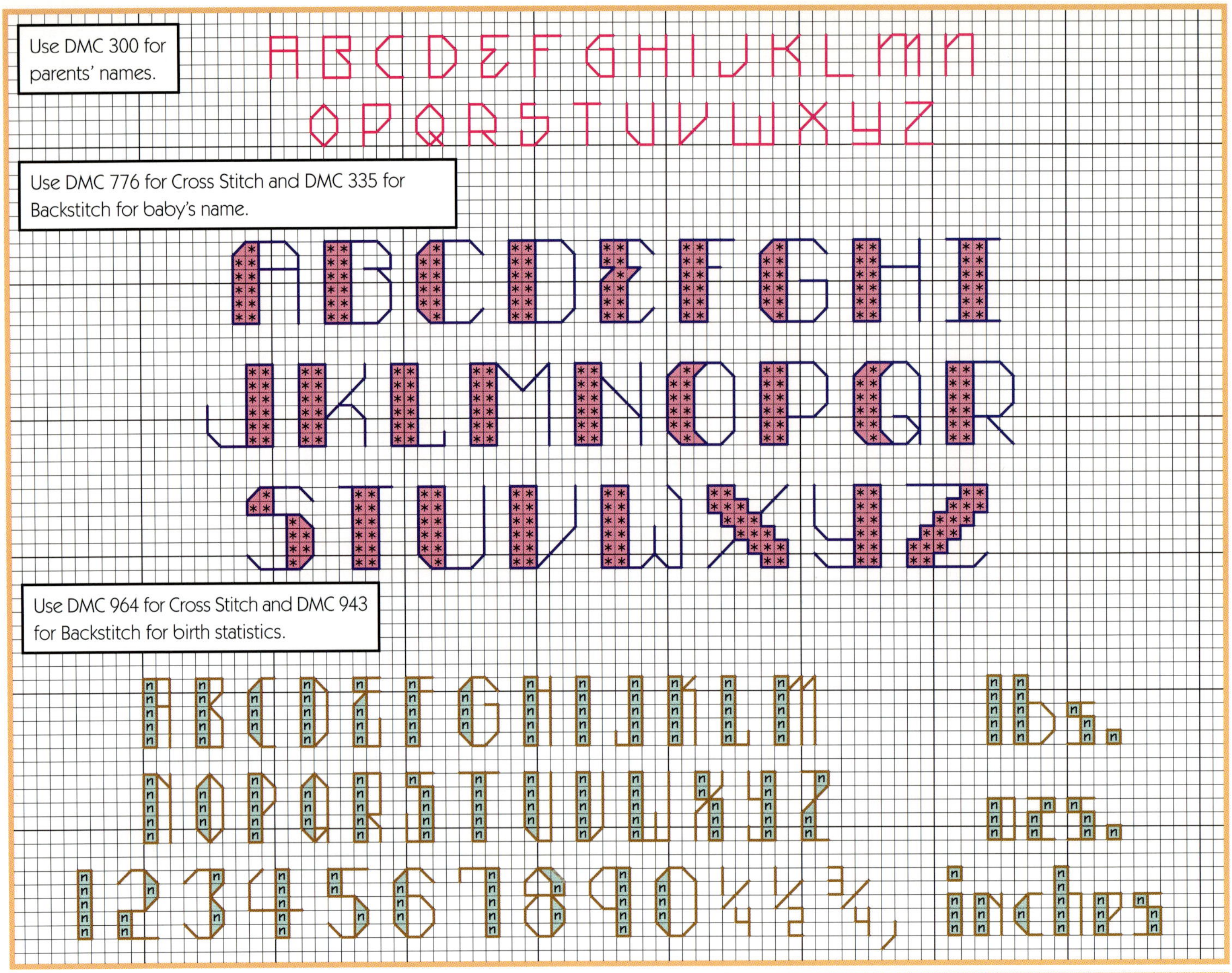

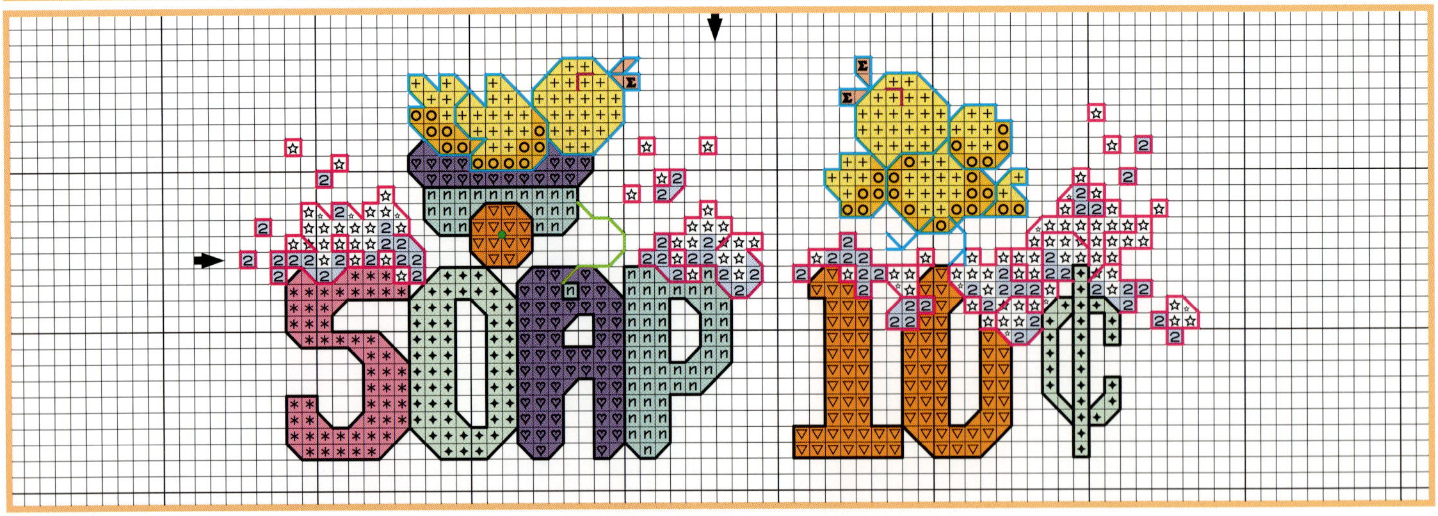

Soap 10¢ (62w x 25h)

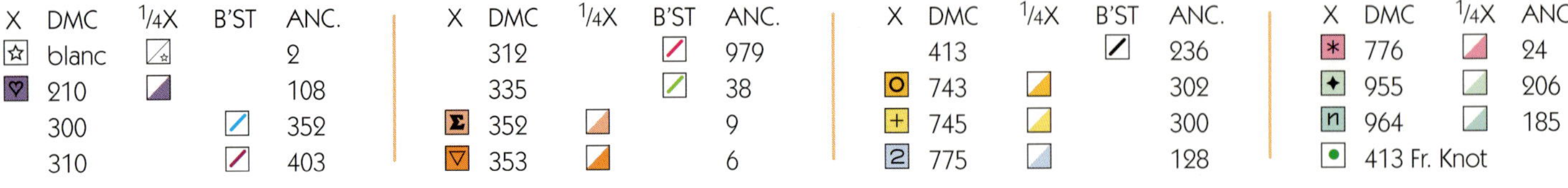

X	DMC	1/4X	B'ST	ANC.
☆	blanc			2
	210			108
	300		╱	352
	310		╱	403

X	DMC	1/4X	B'ST	ANC.
	312		╱	979
	335		╱	38
Σ	352			9
▽	353			6

X	DMC	1/4X	B'ST	ANC.
	413		╱	236
O	743			302
+	745			300
2	775			128

X	DMC	1/4X	ANC.
*	776		24
✦	955		206
n	964		185
•	413 Fr. Knot		

Bath 5¢ (135w x 90h)

DMC	1/4X	B'ST	ANC.
blanc	✓		2
210	✓		108
300		✓	352
310	✓	✓	403
312		✓	979
318	✓		399
335		✓	38
352			9
353	✓		6
402	✓		1047
413		✓	236
436	✓		1045
437	✓		362
563	✓		208
739	✓		387

DMC	1/4X	ANC.
743	✓	302
745	✓	300
762	✓	234
772	✓	259
775	✓	128
776	✓	24
809	✓	130
818	✓	23
945	✓	881
955	✓	206
959	✓	186
964	✓	185
3609	✓	85
3799	✓	236

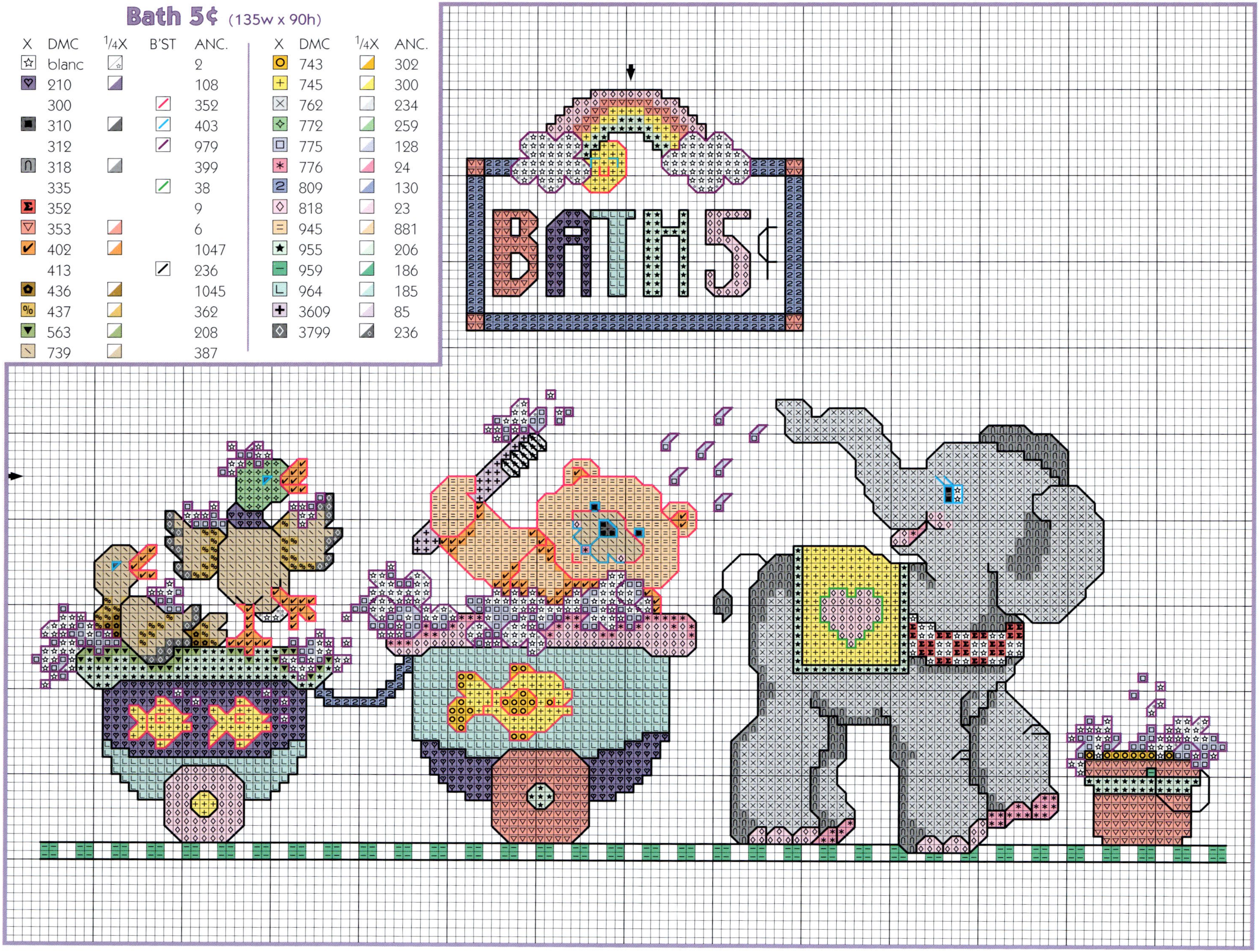

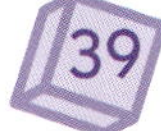

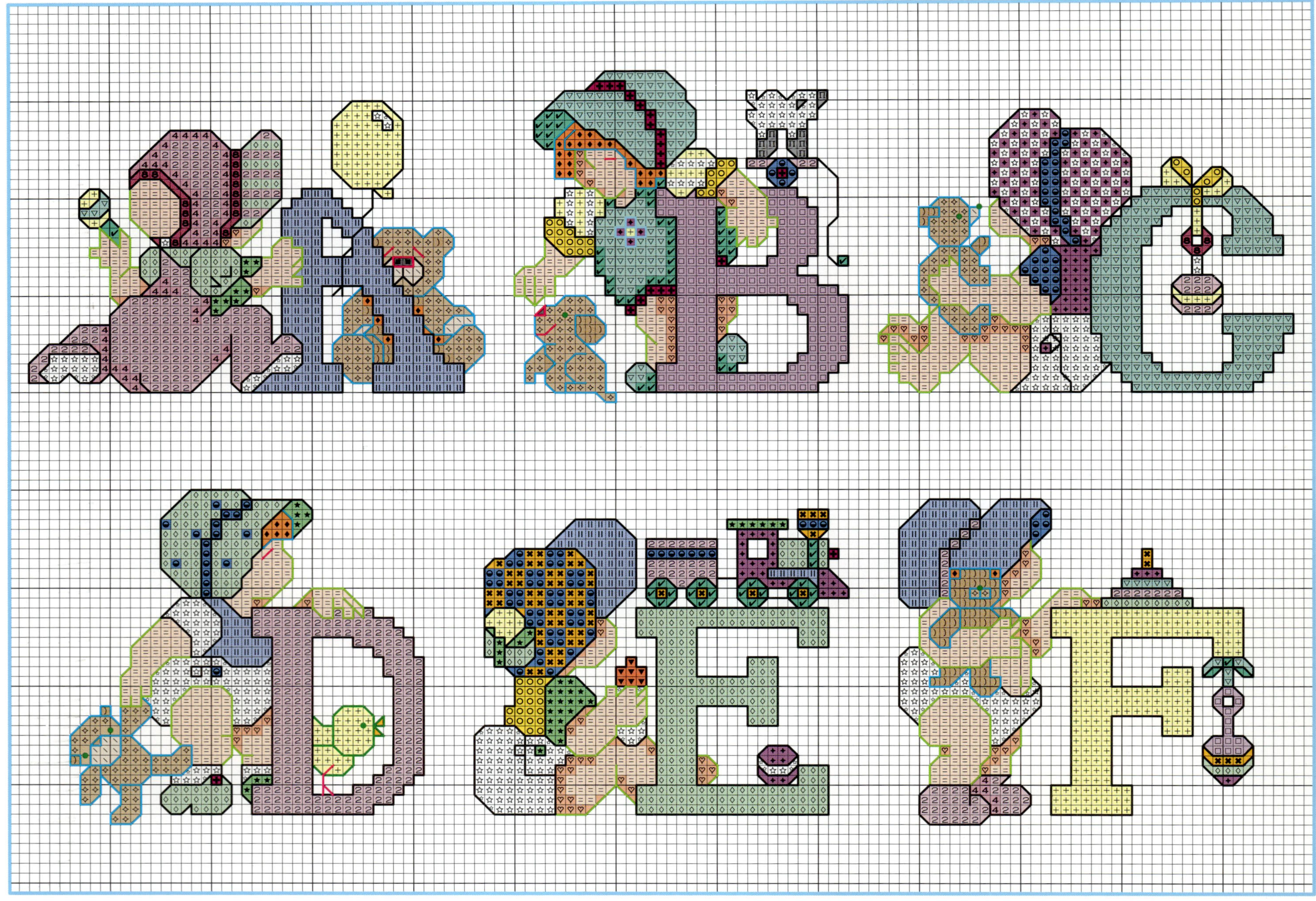

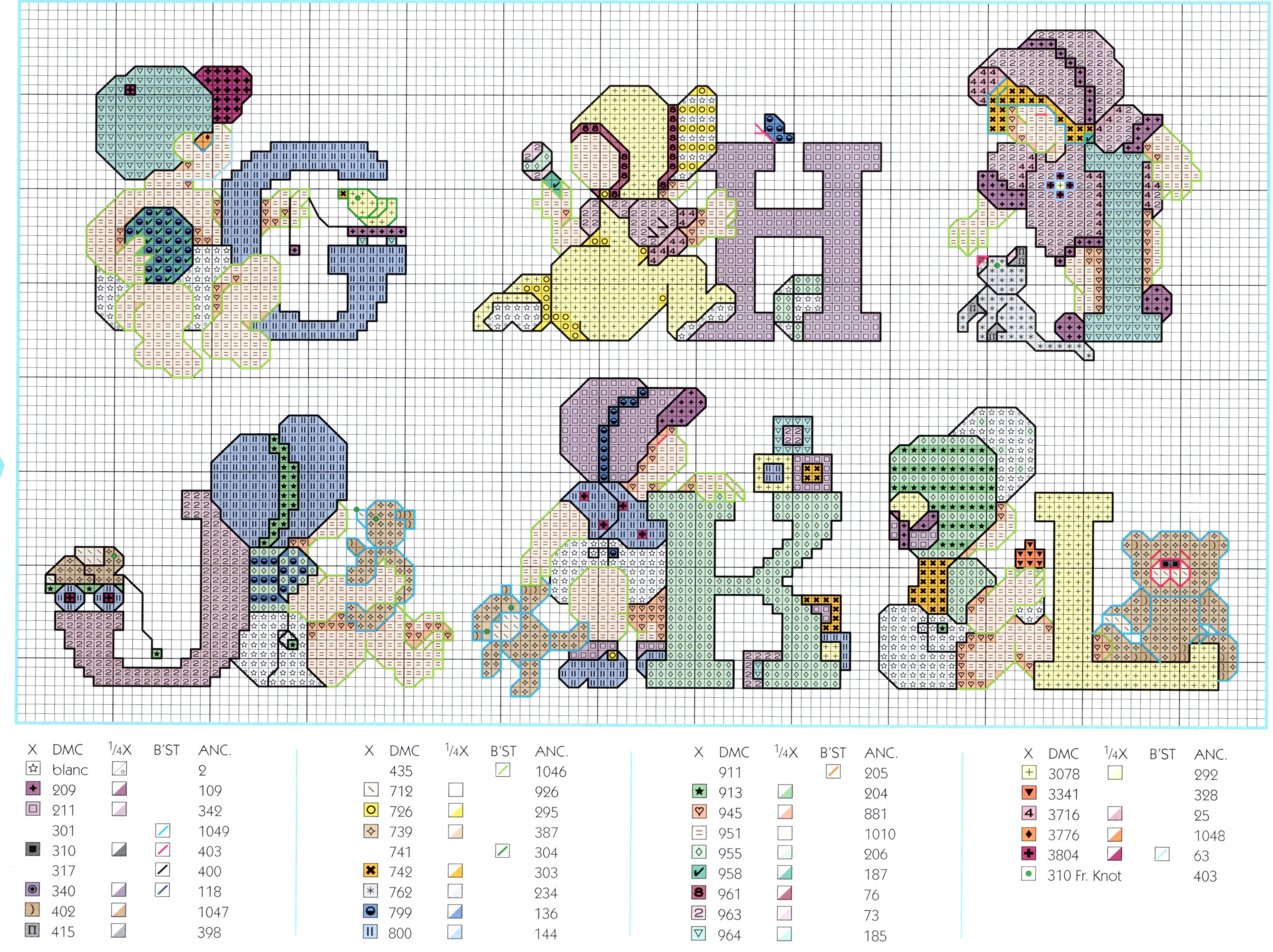

X DMC 1/4X B'ST ANC.
blanc 2
209 109
211 342
301 1049
310 403
317 400
340 118
402 1047
415 398

X DMC 1/4X B'ST ANC.
435 1046
712 926
726 295
739 387
741 304
742 303
762 234
799 136
800 144

X DMC 1/4X B'ST ANC.
911 205
913 204
945 881
951 1010
955 206
958 187
961 76
963 73
964 185

X DMC 1/4X B'ST ANC.
3078 292
3341 328
3716 25
3776 1048
3804 63
310 Fr. Knot 403

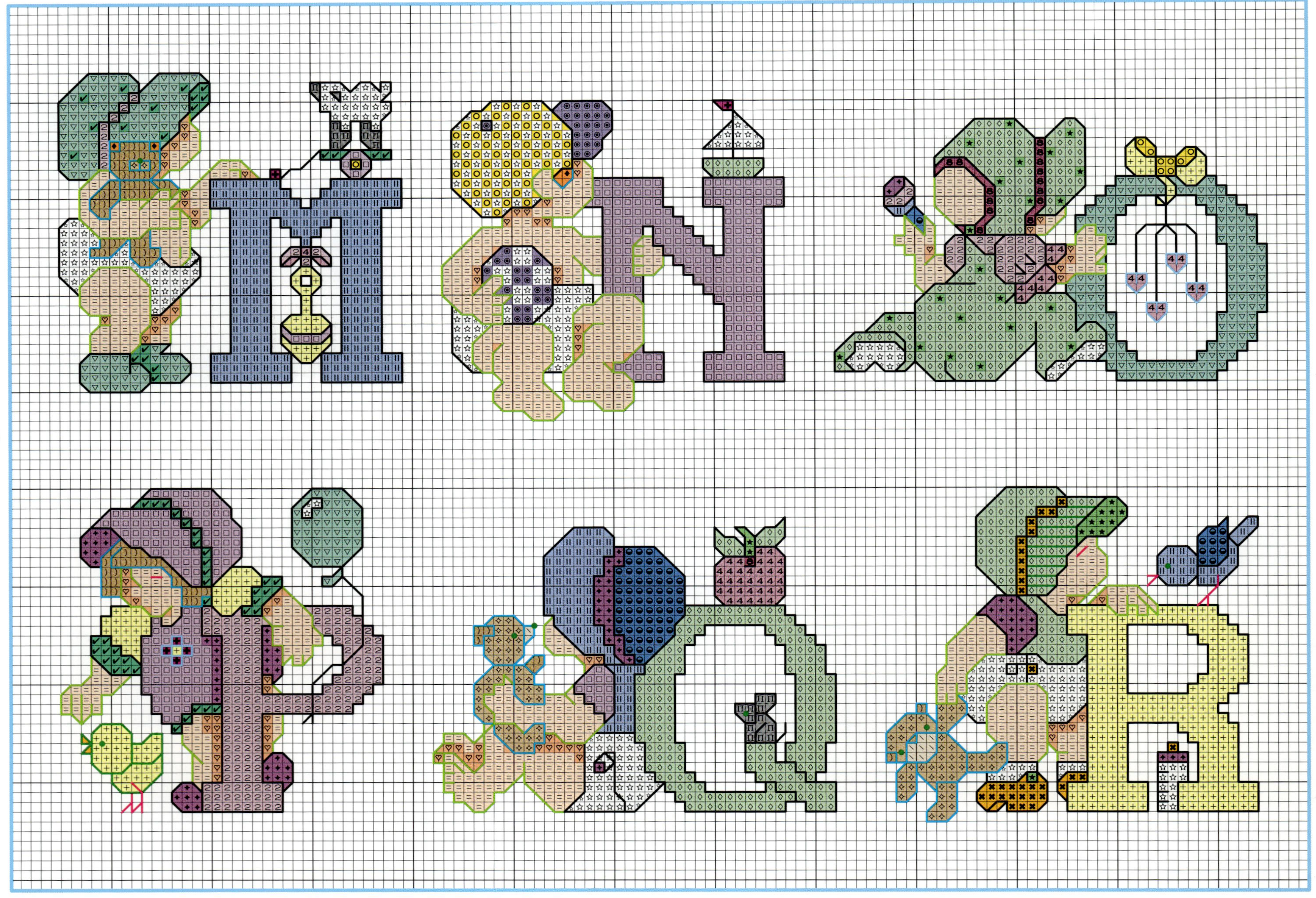

X	DMC	1/4X	B'ST	ANC.
☆	blanc			2
✦	209			109
□	211			342
	301			1049
■	310			403
	317			400
◉	340			118
)	402			1047
Π	415			398

X	DMC	1/4X	B'ST	ANC.
	435			1046
\	712			926
O	726			295
✧	739			387
	741			304
✖	742			303
*	762			234
◒	799			136
II	800			144

X	DMC	1/4X	B'ST	ANC.
	911			205
★	913			204
♡	945			881
=	951			1010
◇	955			206
✔	958			187
8	961			76
2	963			73
▽	964			185

X	DMC	1/4X	B'ST	ANC.
+	3078			292
▼	3341			328
4	3716			25
◆	3776			1048
✚	3804			63
●	310 Fr. Knot			403

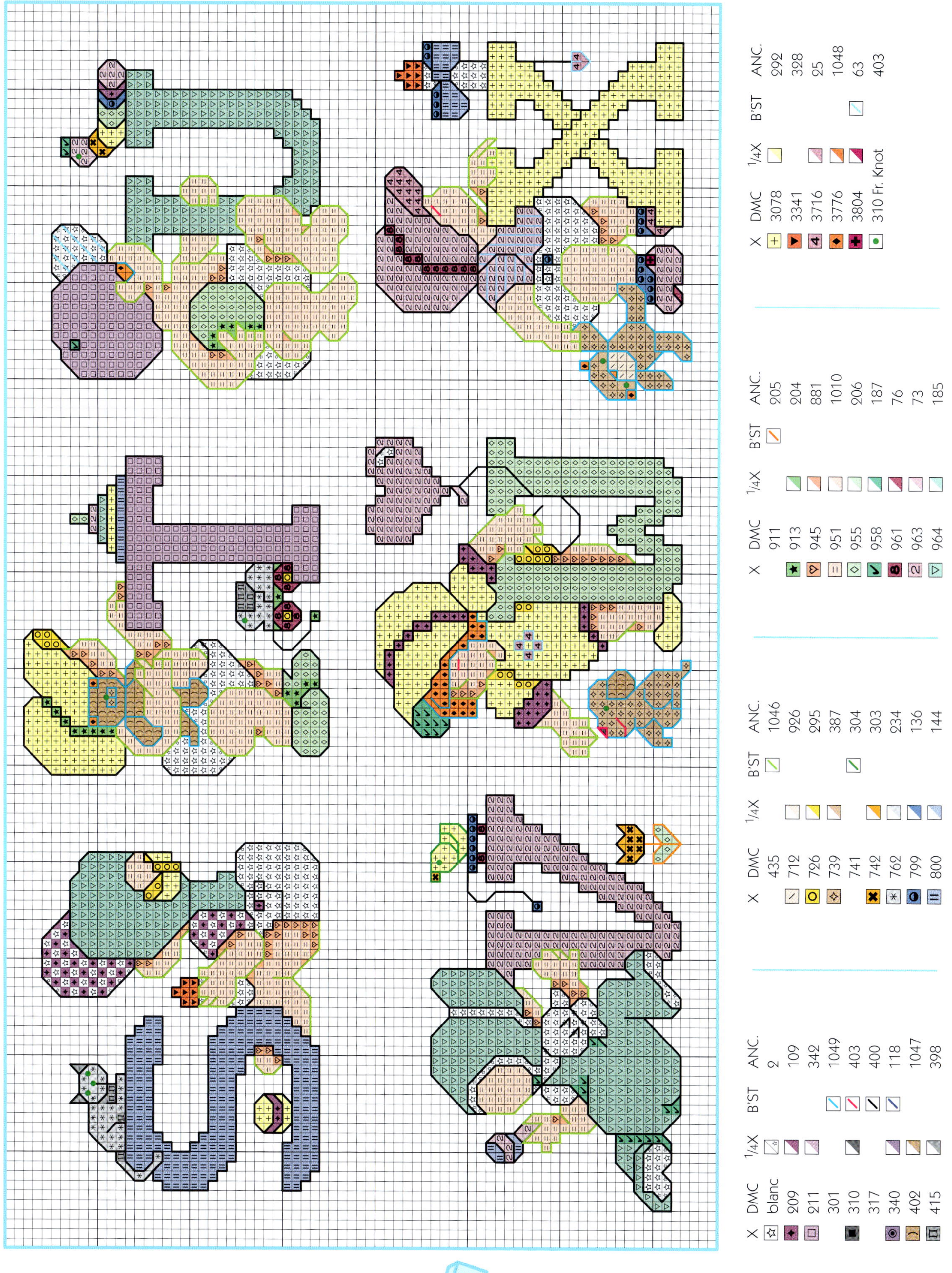

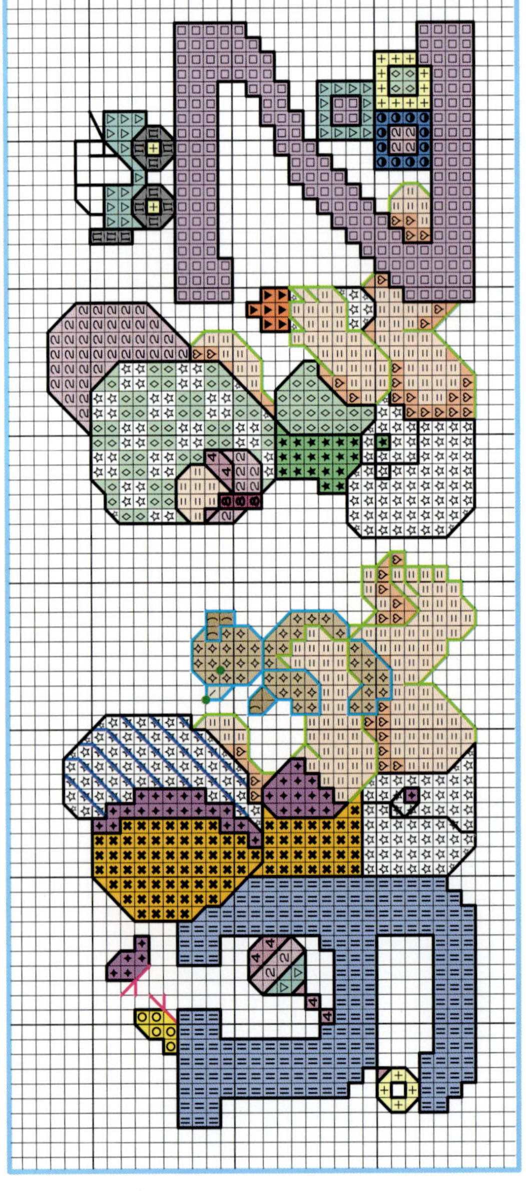

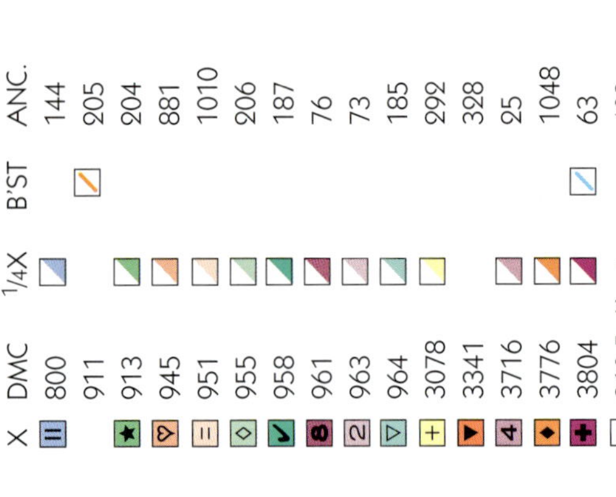

X	DMC	1/4X	B'ST	ANC.
▥	800	◩		144
	911		�—(orange)	205
★	913	◩		204
♥	945	◩		881
‖	951	◩		1010
◇	955	◩		206
◣	958	◩		187
8	961	◩		76
2	963	◩		73
▷	964	◩		185
+	3078	◩		292
▶	3341			328
◀	3716	◩		25
◆	3776	◩		1048
✚	3804	◩	�—(blue)	63
●	310 Fr. Knot			403

X	DMC	1/4X	B'ST	ANC.
☆	blanc	◩		2
◆	209	◩		109
▢	211	◩		342
	301		�—(blue)	1049
■	310	◩	�—(pink)	403
	317		�—(black)	400
◉	340	◩	�—(blue)	118
◡	402	◩		1047
◫	415	◩		398
	435		�—(green)	1046
╱	712	◩		926
○	726	◩		295
◇	739	◩		387
	741		�—(green)	304
✖	742	◩		303
✳	762	◩		234
◑	799	◩		136

X	DMC	1/4X	B'ST	ANC.
☆	blanc	◿		2
	208		◿	110
P	210	◿		108
	301		◿*	1049
■	310	◿	◿	403
	317		◿	400
	335		◿	38
	400		◿†	351
◆	402	◿		1047
d	436	◿		1045
⬟	437	◿		362
	561		◿†	212
♡	738	◿		361
¢	739	◿		387
*	744	◿		301
+	745	◿		300
▣	754	◿		1012
⊠	775	◿		128
◇	776	◿		24
O	800			144
	807		◿*	168
5	809	◿		130
8	818	◿		23
◆	899	◿		52
▼	913			204
△	945	◿		881
>	948	◿		1011
\	955	◿		206
◉	959	◿		186
‖	964	◿		185
2	3825	◿		323

*DMC 301 for flesh, flower, block, and bears. DMC 807 for wording.
†DMC 400 for bears. DMC 561 for leaves.

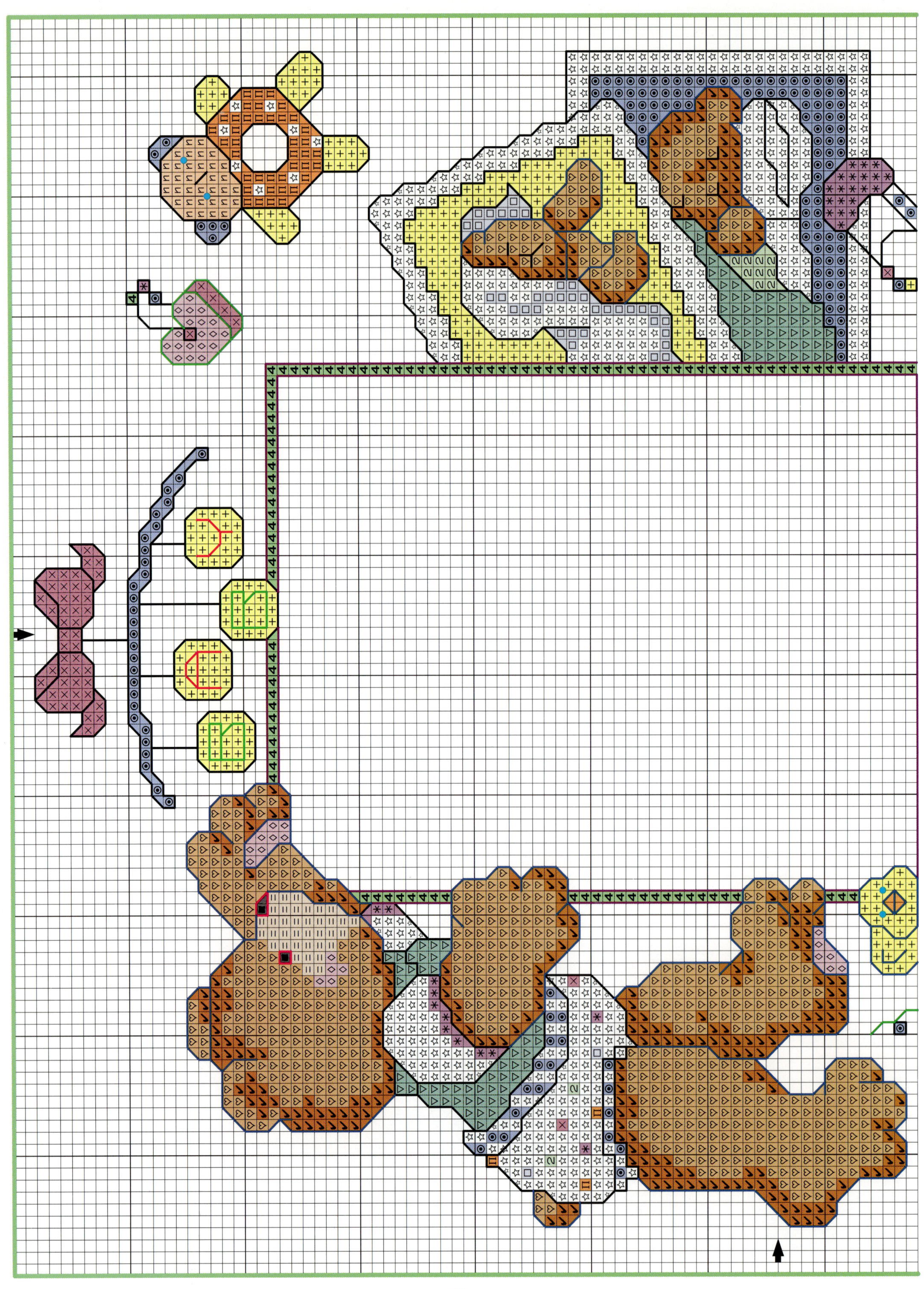

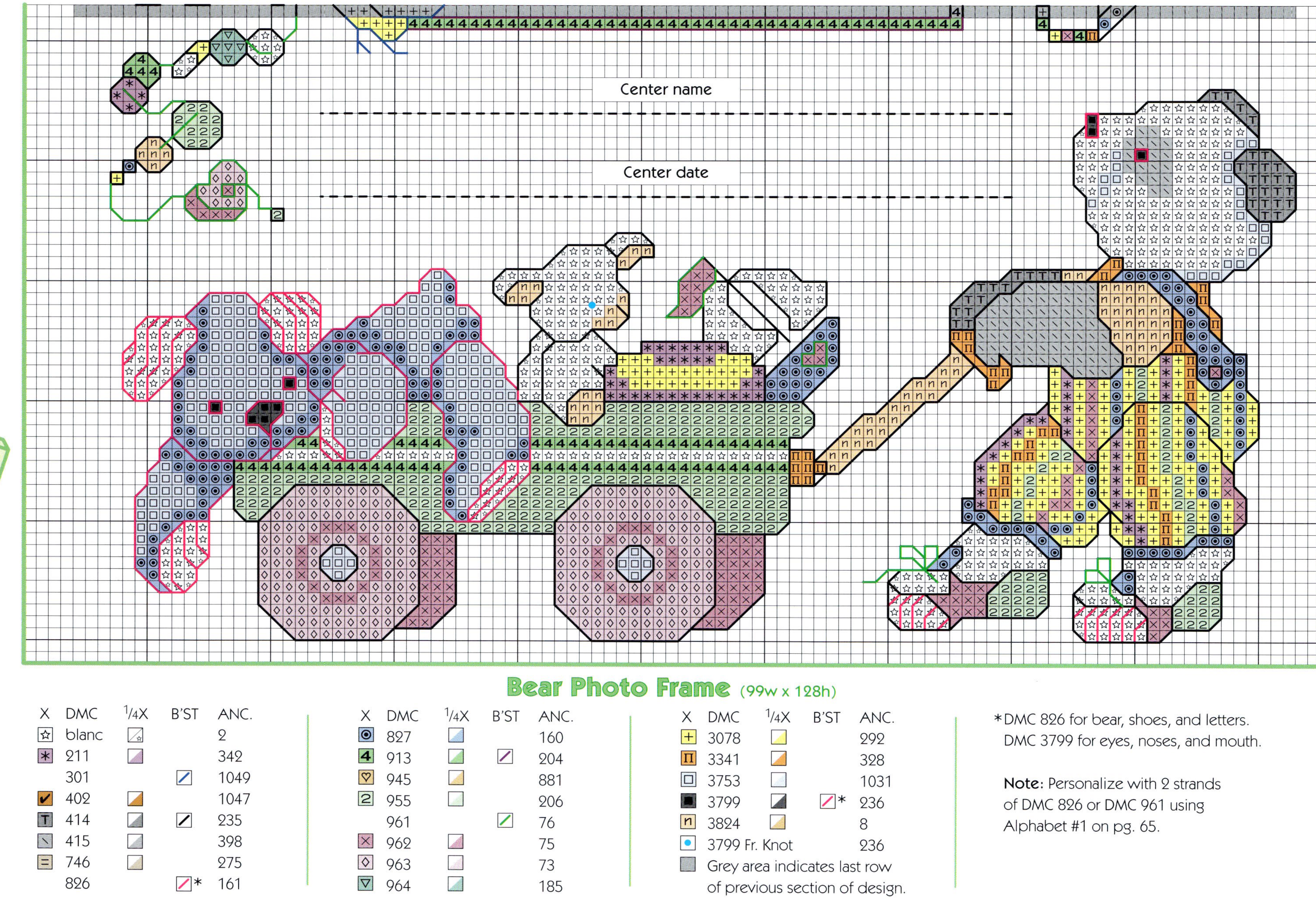

Bear Photo Frame (99w x 128h)

X	DMC	1/4X	B'ST	ANC.
☆	blanc			2
*	211			342
	301		/	1049
✔	402			1047
T	414		/	235
◹	415			398
=	746			275
	826		/*	161

X	DMC	1/4X	B'ST	ANC.
⊙	827			160
4	913		/	204
♡	945			881
2	955			206
	961		/	76
×	962			75
◇	963			73
▽	964			185

X	DMC	1/4X	B'ST	ANC.
+	3078			292
Π	3341			328
□	3753			1031
■	3799		/*	236
n	3824			8
•	3799 Fr. Knot			236
▦	Grey area indicates last row of previous section of design.			

*DMC 826 for bear, shoes, and letters.
DMC 3799 for eyes, noses, and mouth.

Note: Personalize with 2 strands of DMC 826 or DMC 961 using Alphabet #1 on pg. 65.

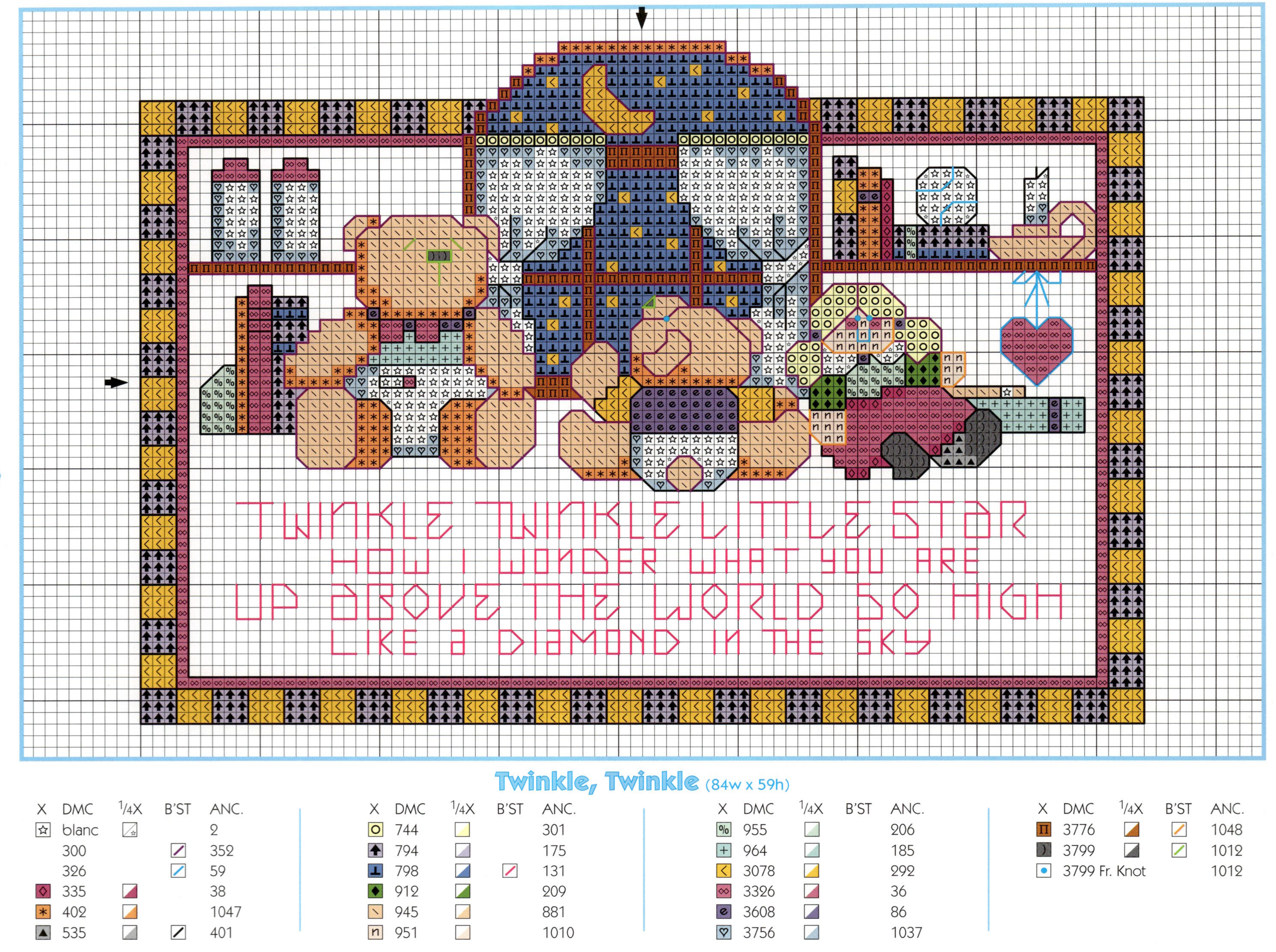

Twinkle, Twinkle (84w x 59h)

X	DMC	1/4X	B'ST	ANC.
☆	blanc			2
	300			352
	326			59
◇	335			38
✳	402			1047
▲	535			401

X	DMC	1/4X	B'ST	ANC.
○	744			301
◄	794			175
⊥	798			131
◆	912			209
	945			881
n	951			1010

X	DMC	1/4X	B'ST	ANC.
%	955			206
+	964			185
	3078			292
∞	3326			36
e	3608			86
♥	3756			1037

X	DMC	1/4X	B'ST	ANC.
Π	3776			1048
◗	3799			1012
•	3799 Fr. Knot			1012

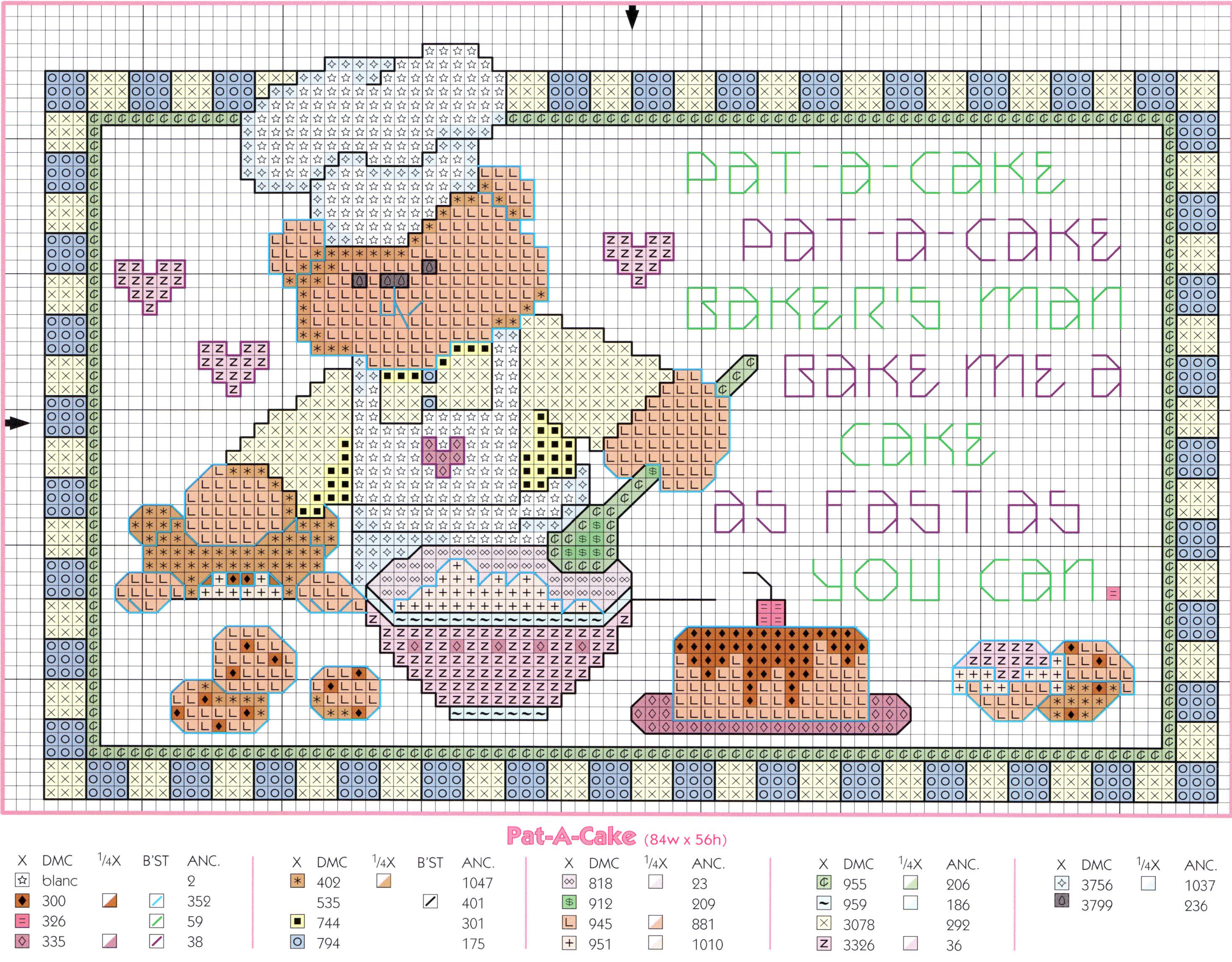

Pat-A-Cake (84w x 56h)

X	DMC	1/4X	B'ST	ANC.
☆	blanc			2
◆	300			352
=	326			59
◇	335			38

X	DMC	1/4X	B'ST	ANC.
*	402			1047
	535			401
■	744			301
⊙	794			175

X	DMC	1/4X	ANC.
⊗	818		23
$	912		209
L	945		881
+	951		1010

X	DMC	1/4X	ANC.
¢	955		206
~	959		186
×	3078		292
Z	3326		36

X	DMC	1/4X	ANC.
◇	3756		1037
◐	3799		236

Gardening Bunnies
(169w x 124h)

X	DMC	¼X	B'ST	ANC.
☆	blanc			2
✕	210			108
	300		✓	352
■	310	✓	✓	403
d	351	✓		10
+	352	✓		9
2	369	✓		1043
U	402	✓	✓	1047
	414		✓	235
>	415	✓		398
e	743			302
(	745	✓		300
*	746			275
✕	762	✓		234
◆	775	✓		128
4	813	✓		161
	826		✓	161
	899		✓	52
♠	912	✓	✓	209
m	920			1004
=	945	✓		881
♡	955	✓		206
‡	958			187
□	963	✓		73
↑	964			185
⚓	3326	✓		36
∞	3607	✓		87
>	3609	✓		85
∩	3756			1037
H	3776	✓		1048
•	310 Fr. Knot			403

Note: Personalize using alphabet and numbers provided.

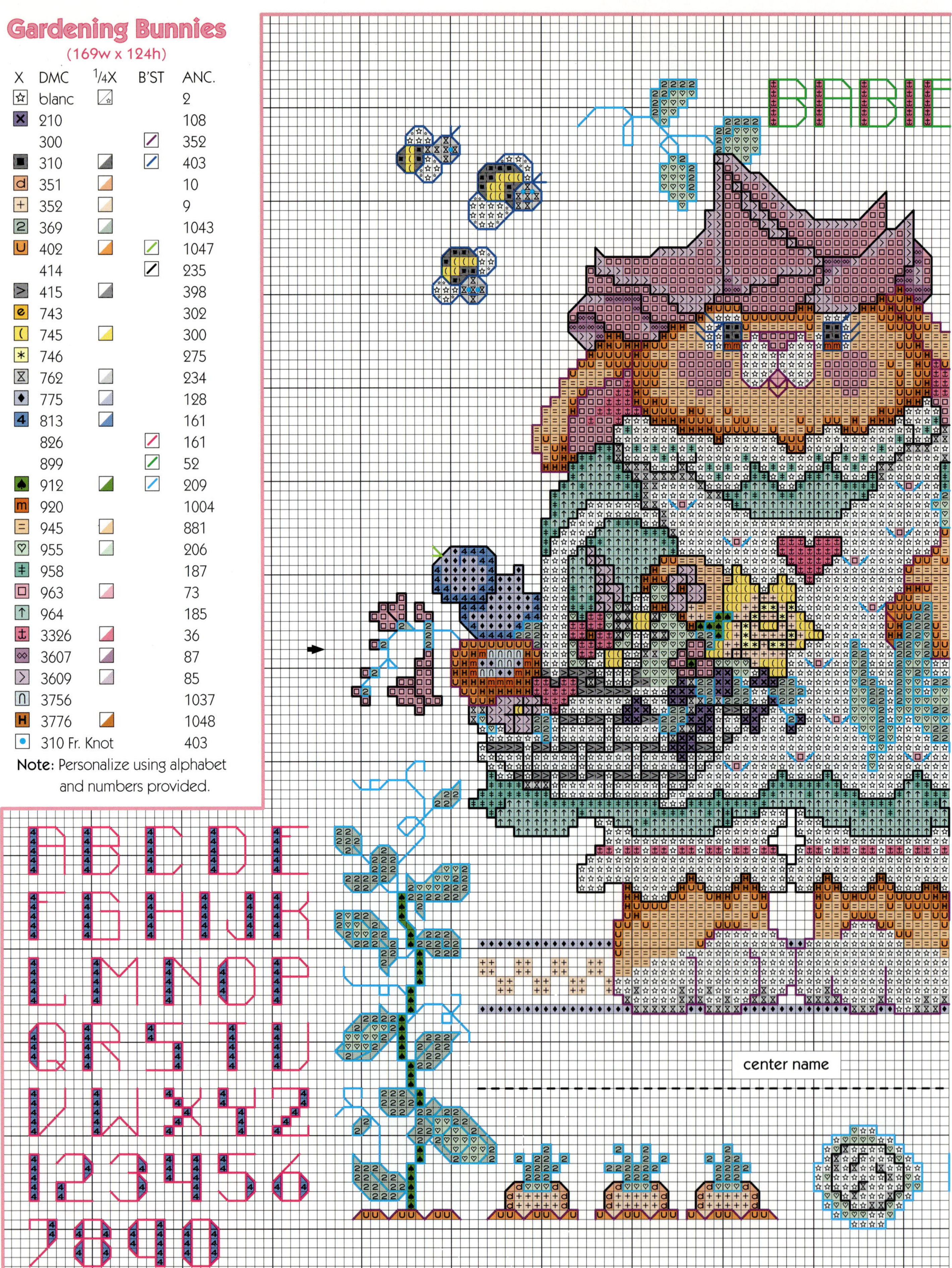

ABCDE
FGHIJK
LMNOP
QRSTU
VWXYZ
123456
7890

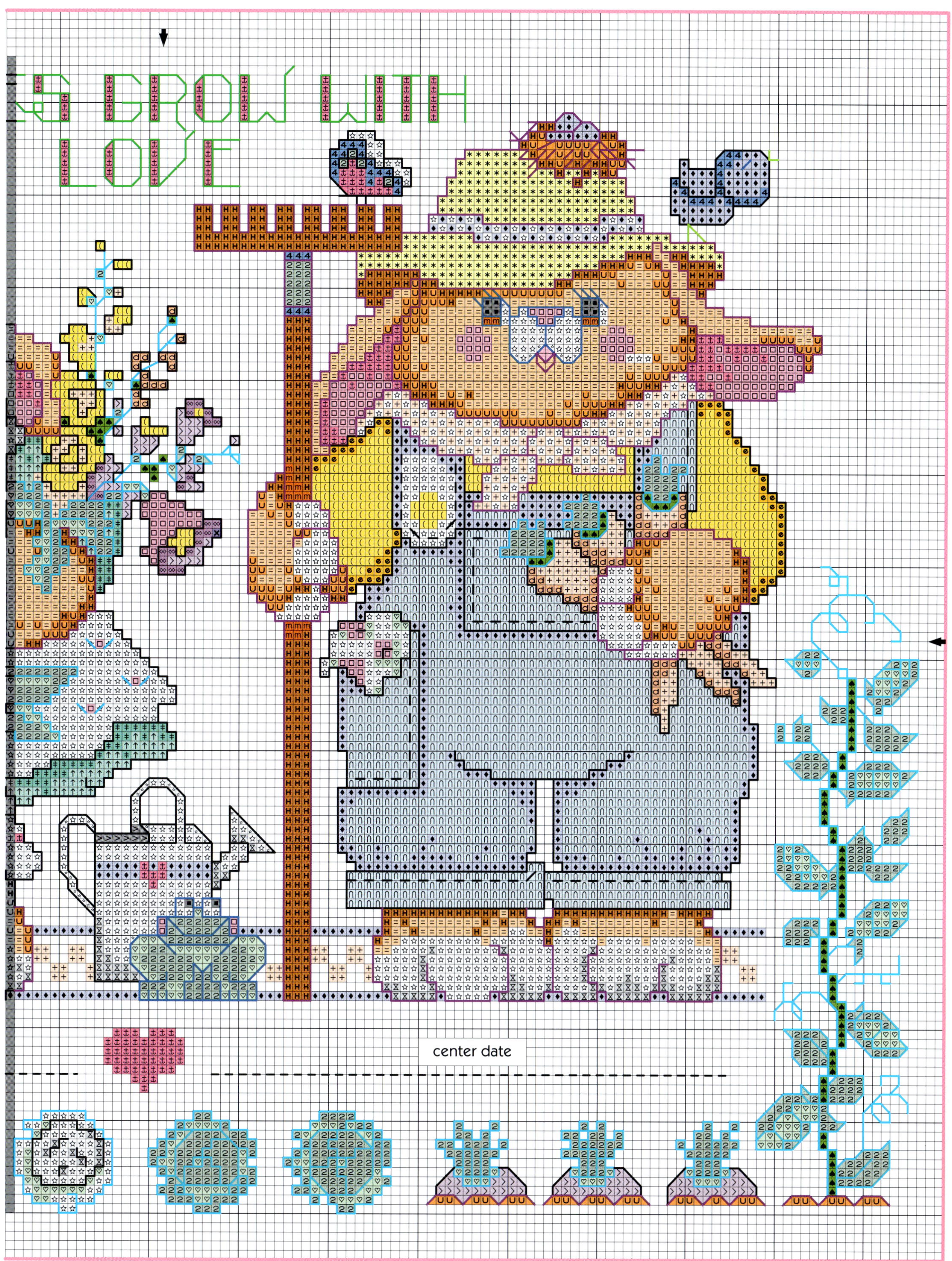
S GROW WITH
LOVE
center date

X	DMC	¼X	B'ST	ANC.
☆	blanc			2
⊠	210			108
⧻	211			342
★	322		◢	978
◣	335			38
	413		◢	236
❭	647			1040
✳	722		◢*	323
﹪	738			361
(	743			302
＋	744			301
＼	762			234
2	775			128
◥	813			161
◆◆	912			209
¢	951			1010
↑	955			206
✔	959			186
△	963			73
◉	964			185
	975		◢	355
H	3326			36
♥	3607			87
⋈	3609			85
■	3799		◢	236

☐ Grey area indicates last row
of previous section of design.

＊Use **2** strands of floss.

Note: Personalize using alphabet
and numbers provided.

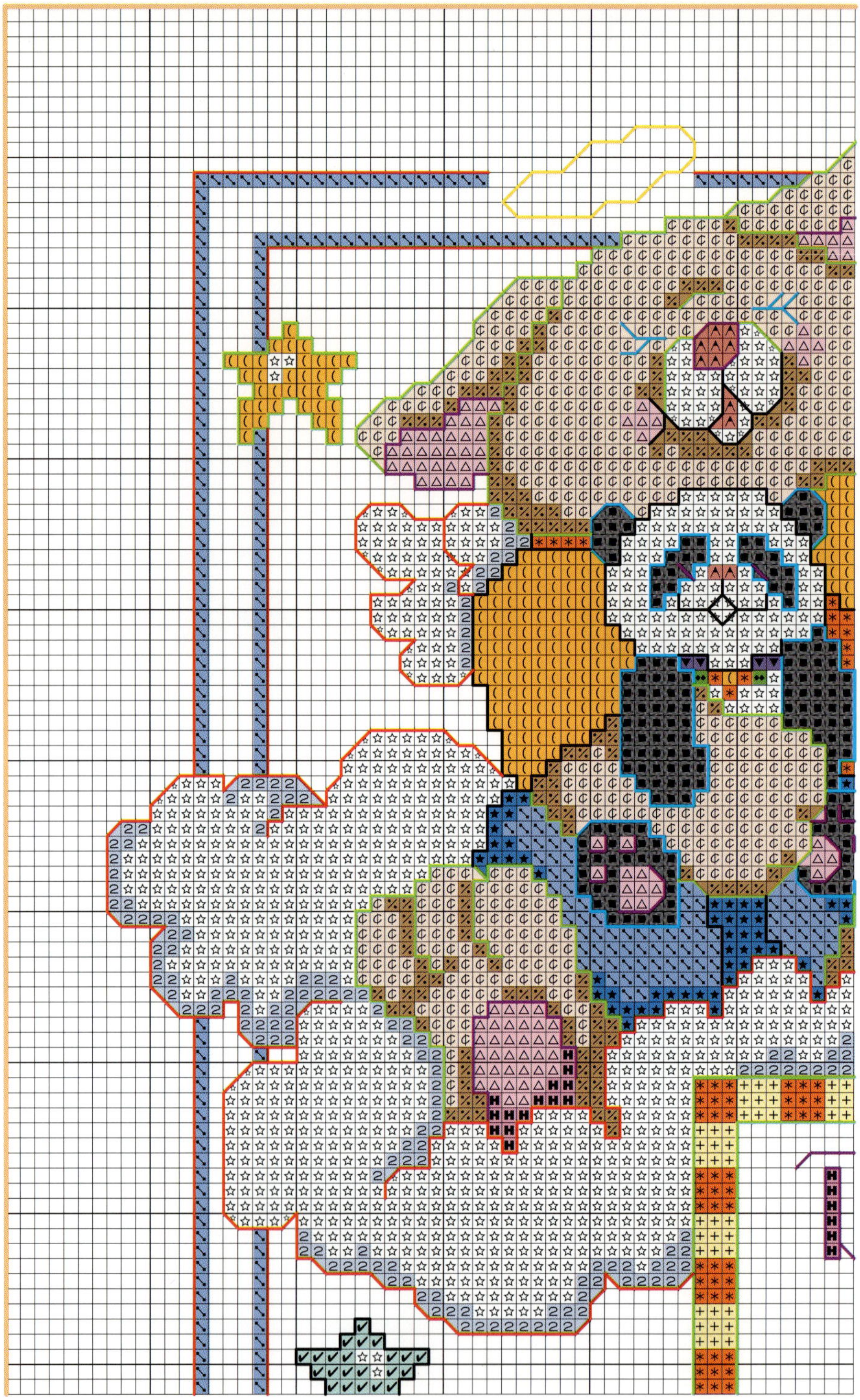

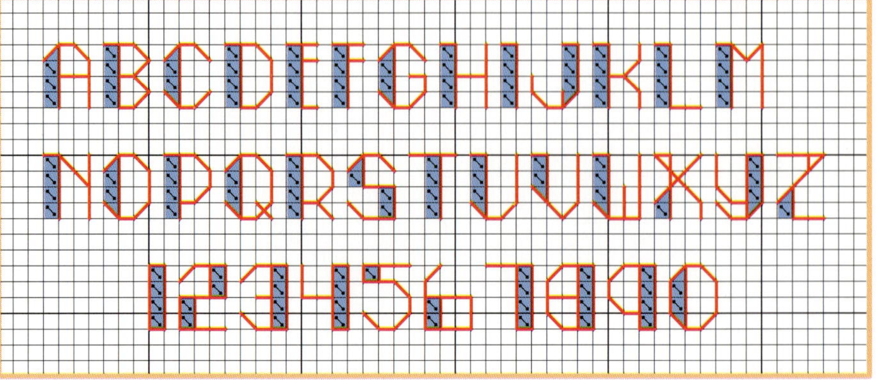

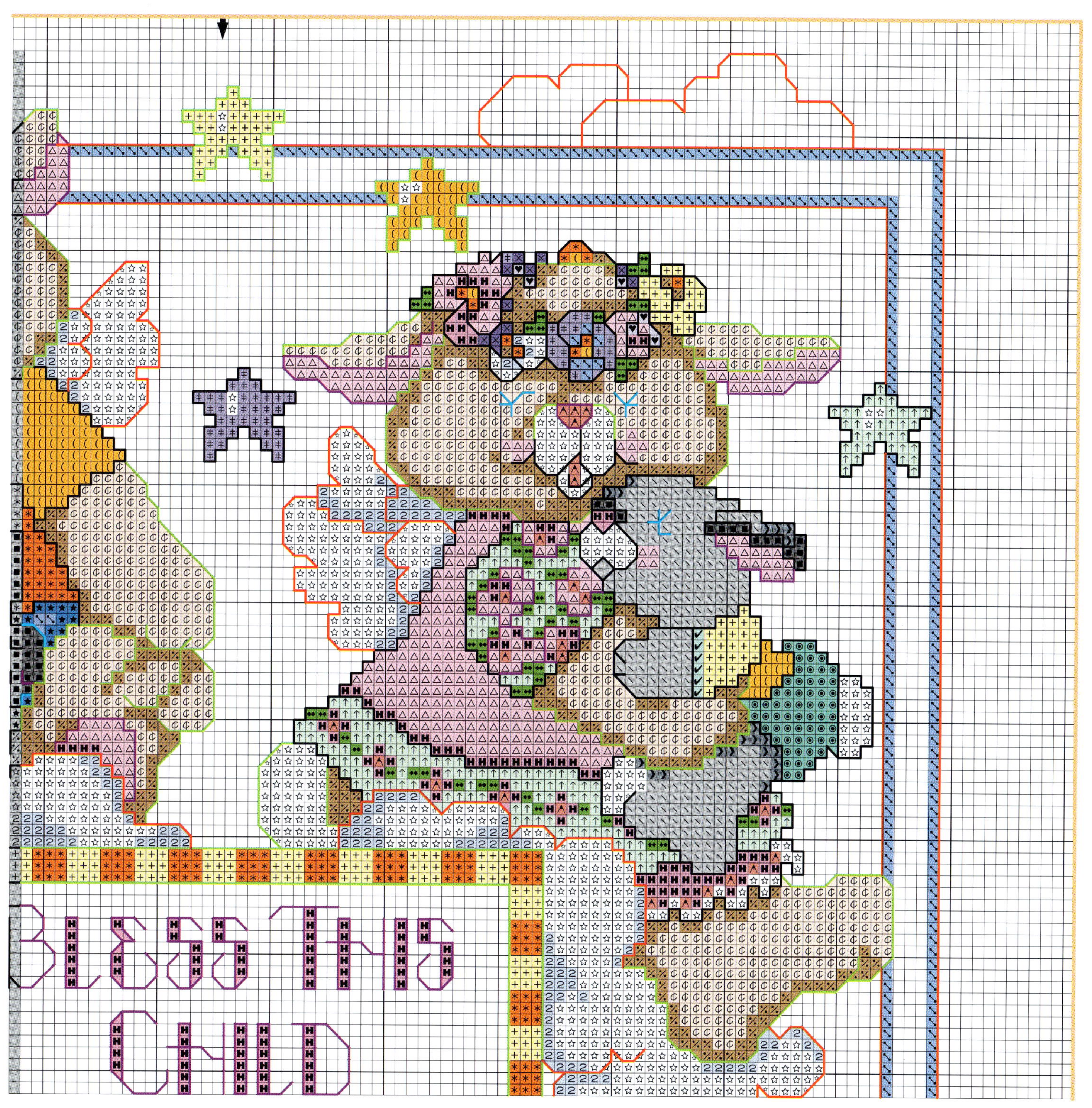

BLESS THIS
CHILD

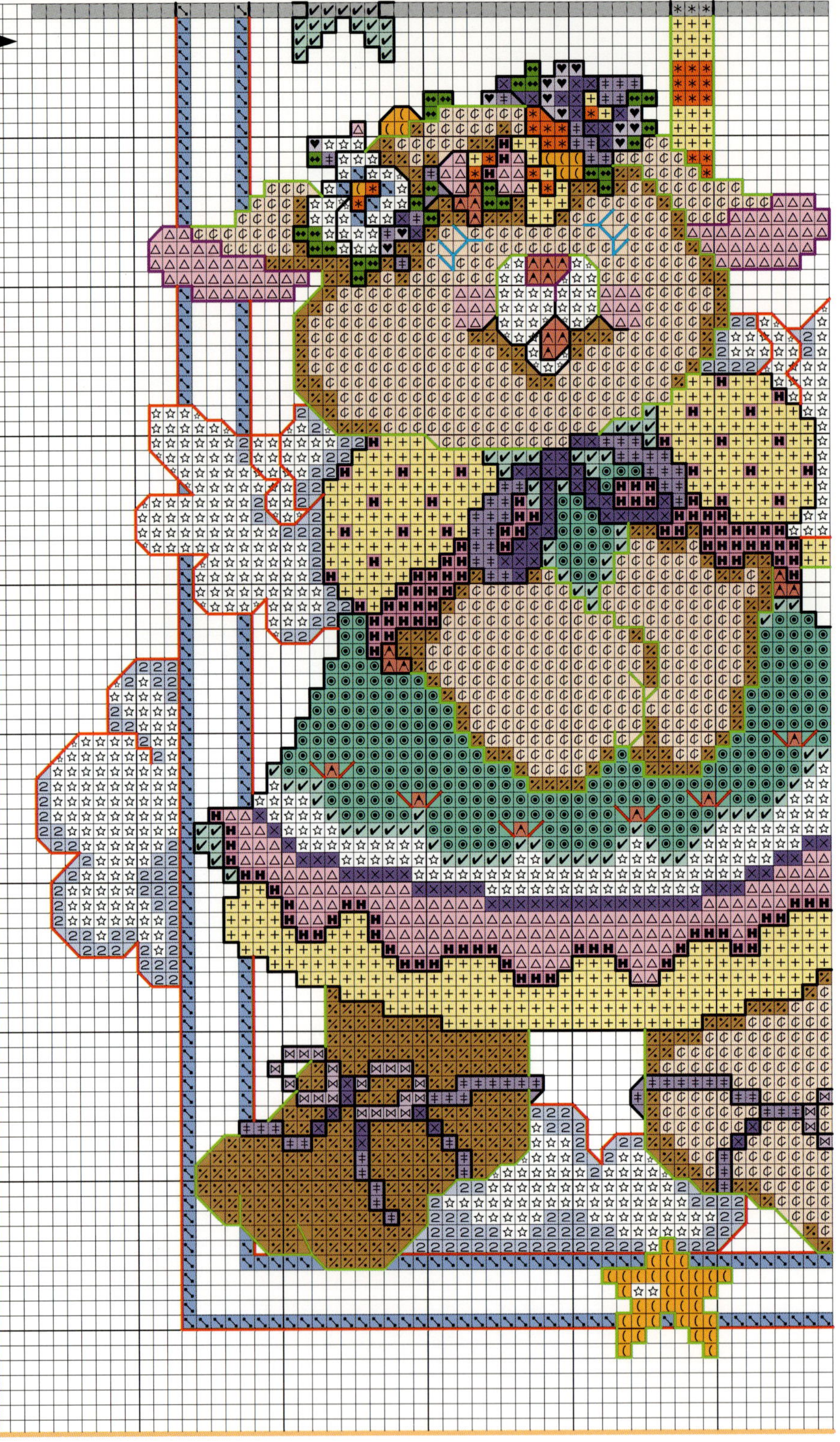

Heavenly Bunnies
(145w x 181h)

X	DMC	¼X	B'ST	ANC.
☆	blanc			2
✕	210			108
‡	211			342
★	322		◿	978
⌂	335		◿	38
	413		◿	236
❱	647			1040
✳	722		◿*	323
⁒	738			361
(	743			302
+	744			301
	762			234
2	775			128
↘	813			161
◆	912			209
₵	951			1010
↑	955			206
✔	959			186
△	963			73
◉	964			185
	975		◿	355
H	3326			36
♥	3607			87
⊠	3609			85
■	3799		◿	236

▢ Grey area indicates last row of previous section of design.

* Use **2** strands of floss.

Note: Personalize using alphabet and numbers provided.

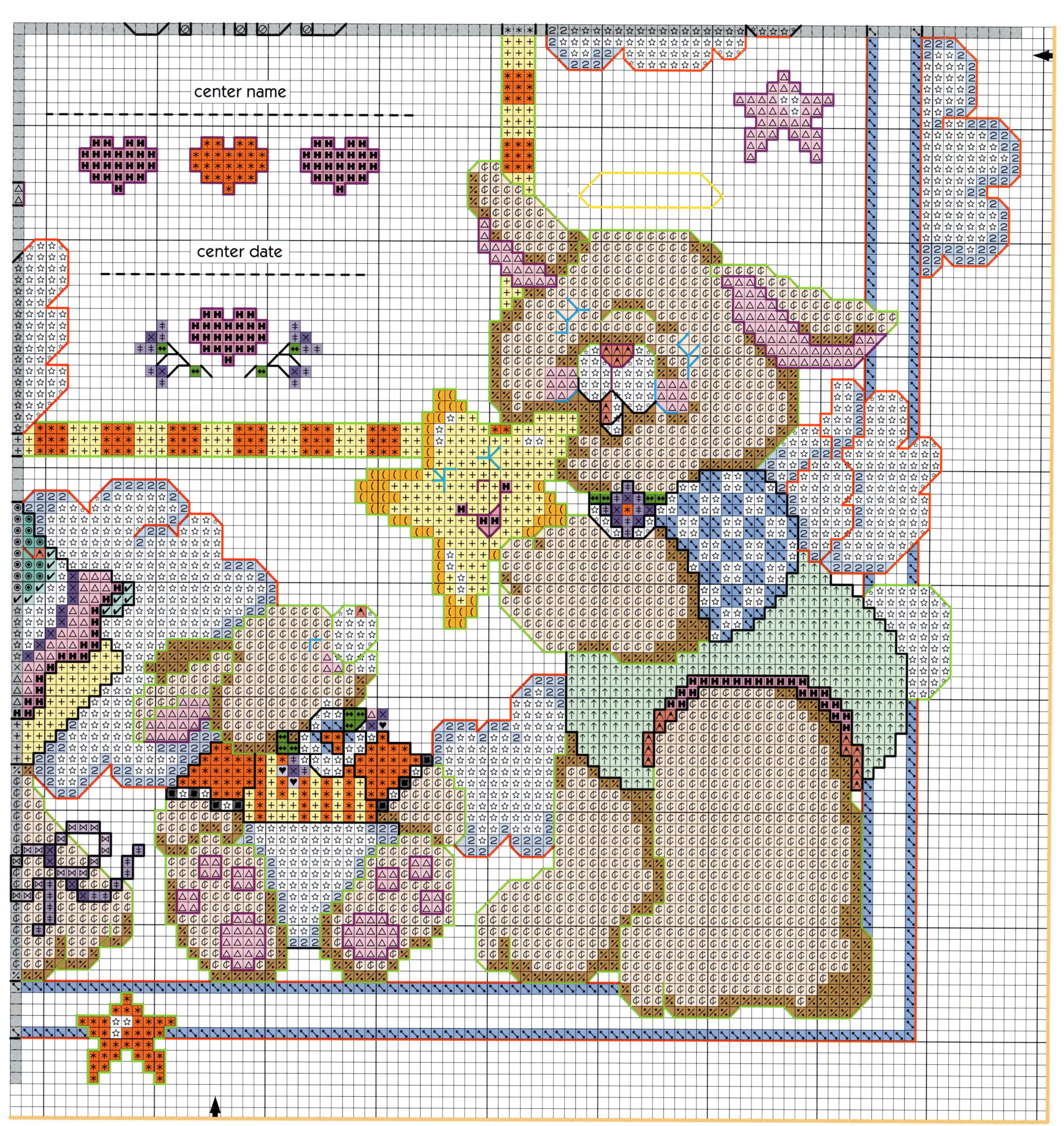
center name
center date

Welcome Baby
(167w x 134h)

X	DMC	ANC.	B'ST	¼X
	blanc	2		
	310	403		
	352	9		
	369	1043		
	402	1047		
	535	401		
	561	212		
	563	208		
	738	361		
	739	387		
	743	302		
	745	300		
	775	128		
	801	359		
	813	161		
	818	23		
	826	161		
	839	1086		
	841	1082		
	842	1080		
	921	1003		
	945	881		
	958	187		
	964	185		
	3326	36		
	3607	87		
	3609	85		
	3756	1037		
	801 Fr. Knot	359		

Note: Personalize with DMC 813 for Cross Stitch and DMC 826 for Backstitch using Alphabet #2 on pg. 65.

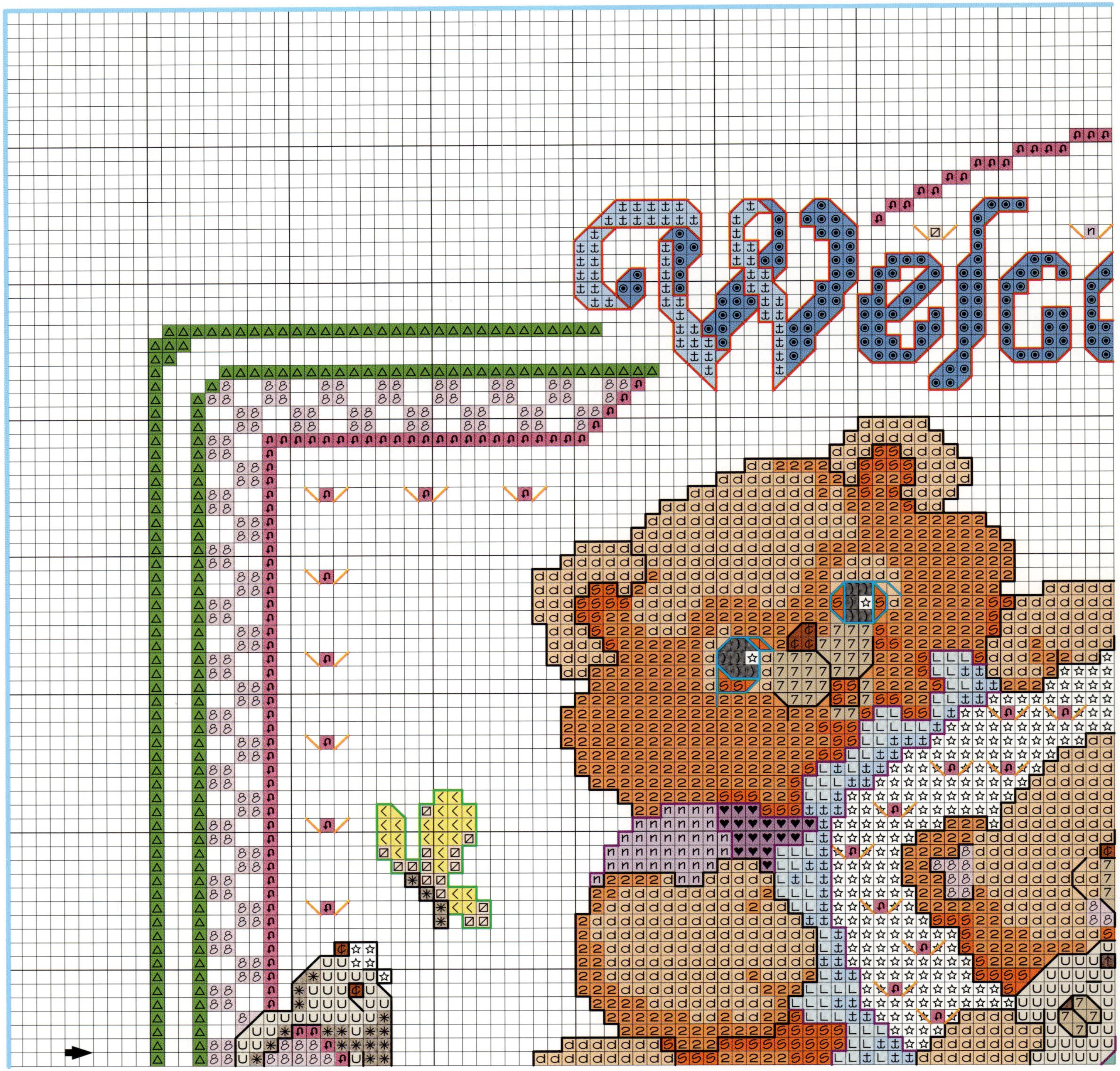

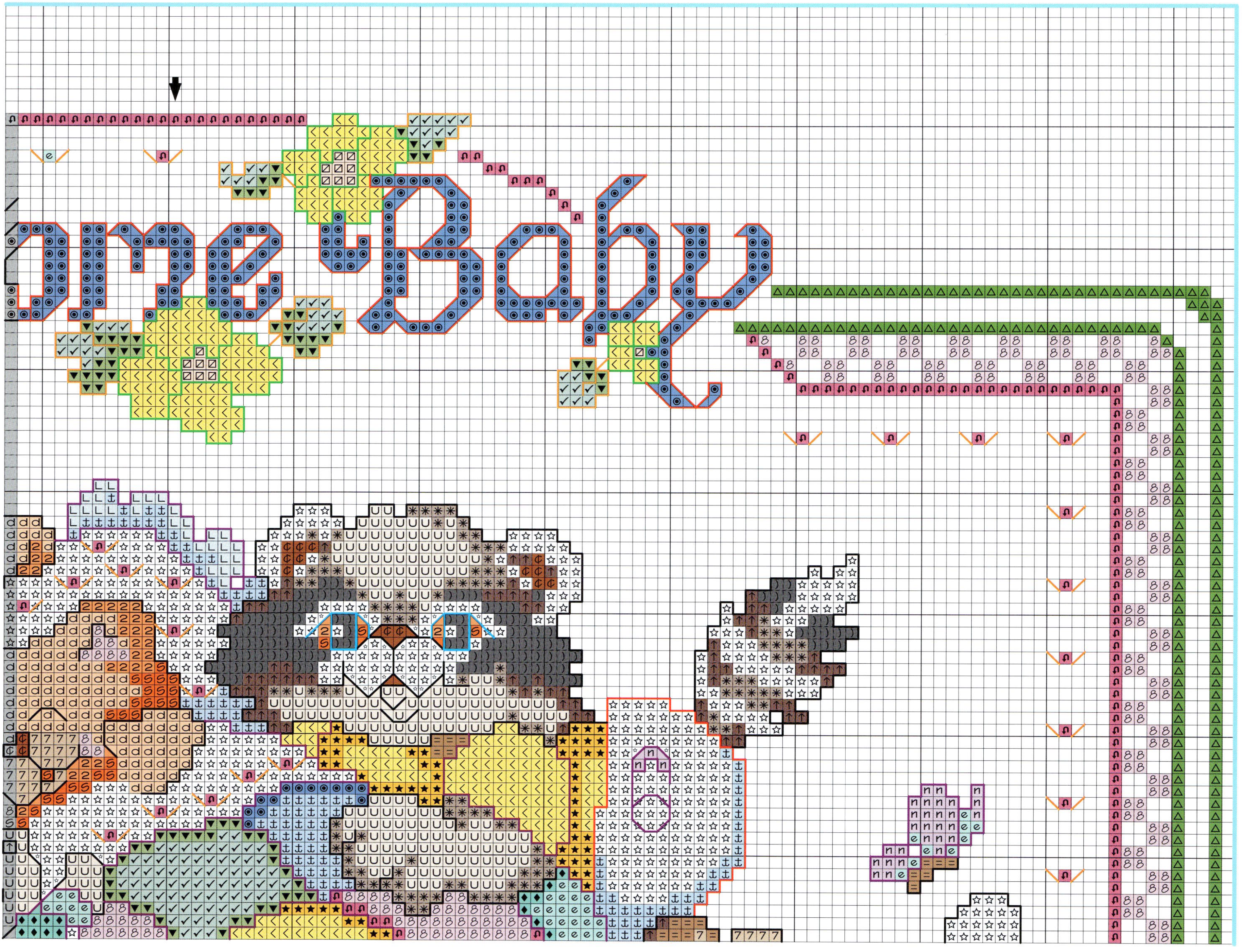
ome Baby

Welcome Baby
(167w x 134h)

X	DMC	1/4X	B'ST	ANC.
☆	blanc	☆		2
	310		╲	403
	352			9
	369			1043
	402			1047
	535		╲	401
	561		╲	212
	563			208
	738			361
	739			387
	743			302
	745			300
	775			128
	801		╲	359
	813			161
	818			23
	826		╲	161
	839			1086
	841			1082
	842			1080
	921		╲	1003
	945			881
	958			187
	964			185
	3326			36
	3607			87
	3609			85
	3756			1037
•	801 Fr. Knot			359

Note: Personalize with DMC 813 for Cross Stitch and DMC 826 for Backstitch using Alphabet #2 on pg. 65.

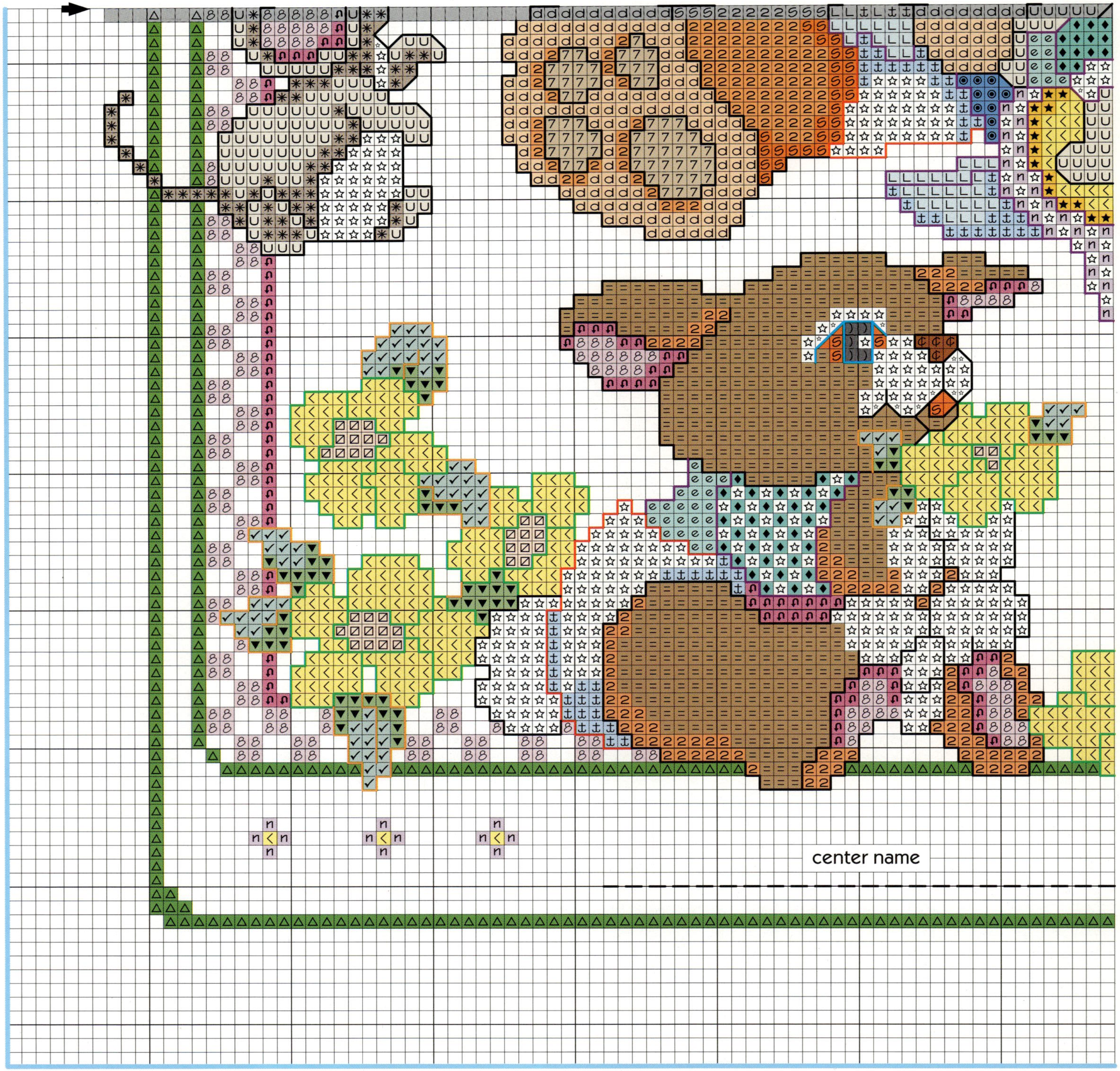

center name

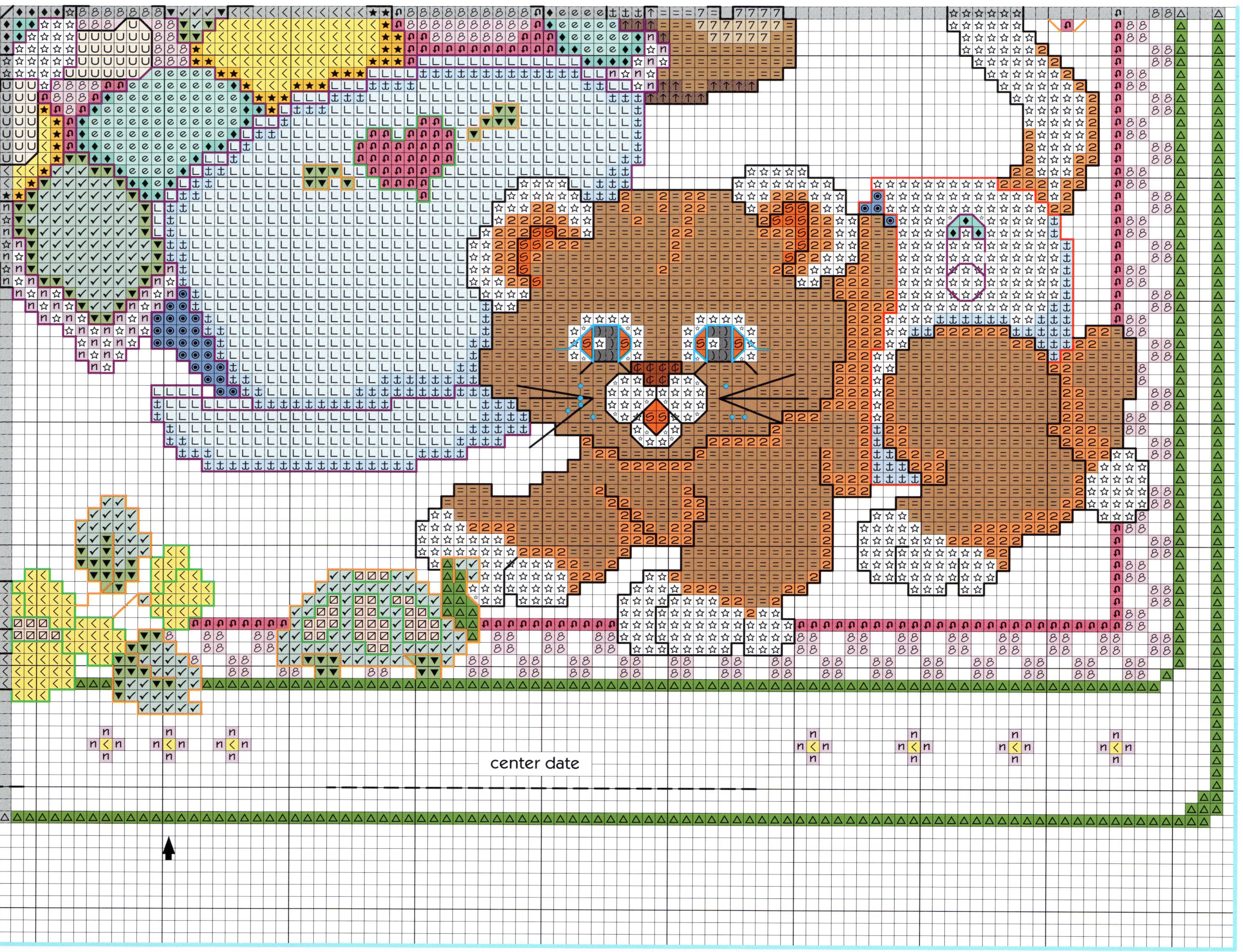
center date

How to Read Charts

Each chart is made up of a key and a gridded design where each square represents a stitch. The symbols in the key tell which floss color to use for each stitch in the chart. The following headings and symbols are given:

X — Cross Stitch
DMC — DMC color number
¼ X — Quarter Stitch
B'ST — Backstitch
ANC. — Anchor color number

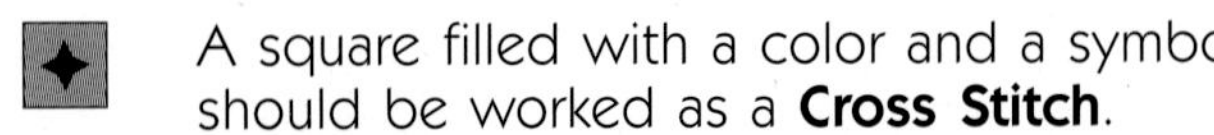

A square filled with a color and a symbol should be worked as a **Cross Stitch**.

A triangle should be worked as a **Quarter Stitch**.

A straight line should be worked as a **Backstitch**.

A large dot listed near the end of the key should be worked as a **French Knot**.

In the chart, the symbol for a **Cross Stitch** may be omitted when a **Backstitch** crosses its square.

How to Stitch

Always work **Cross Stitches** and **Quarter Stitches** first and then add the **Backstitch** and **French Knots**.

Cross Stitch (X): For horizontal rows, work stitches in two journeys *(Fig. 1)*. For vertical rows, complete each stitch as shown *(Fig. 2)*. When working over two fabric threads, work Cross Stitch as shown in **Fig. 3**.

Fig. 1   **Fig. 2**

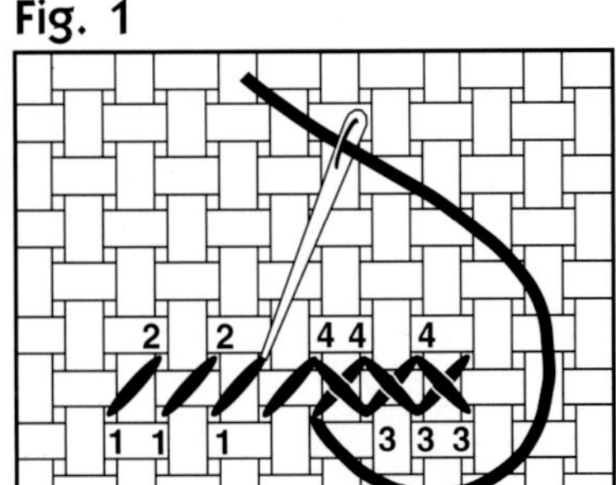
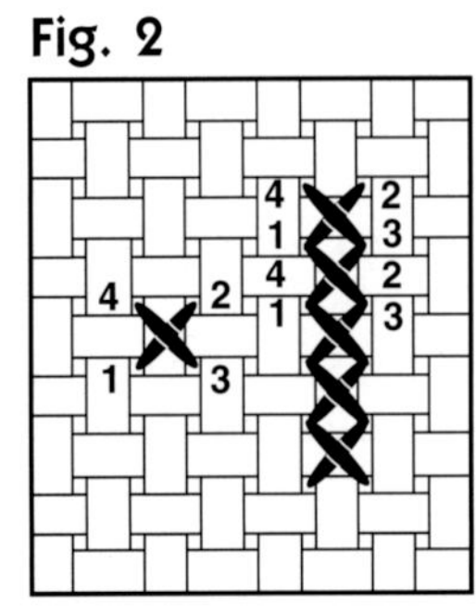

Fig. 3

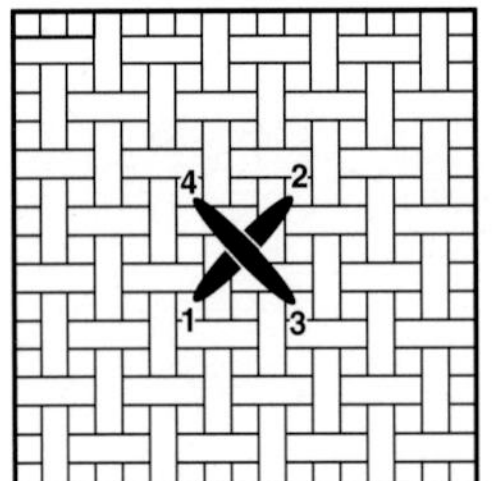

Quarter Stitch (¼X): Come up at 1 *(Fig. 4)*, then split fabric thread to go down at 2. **Fig. 5** shows the technique for Quarter Stitch when working over two fabric threads.

Fig. 4   **Fig. 5**

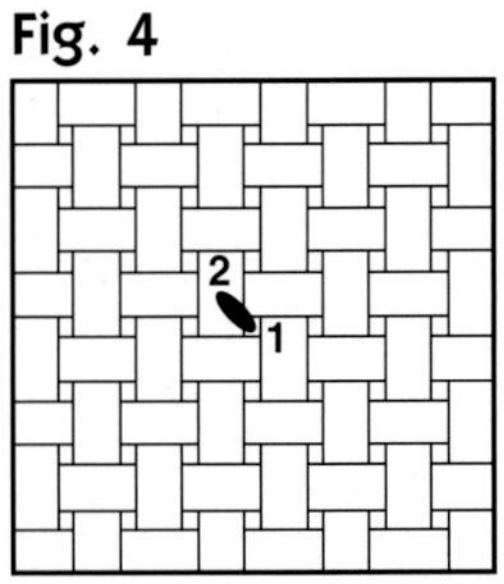
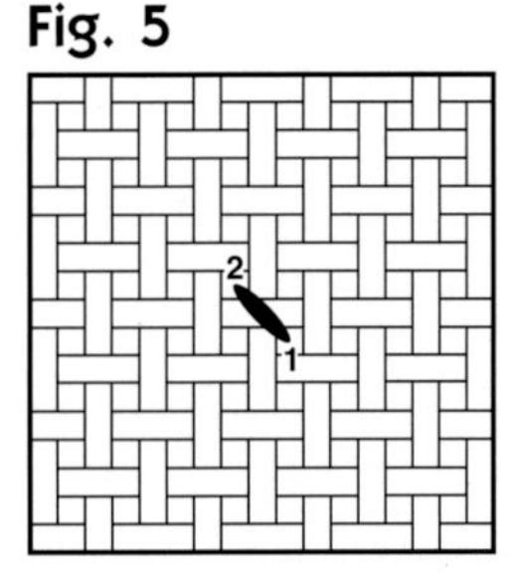

Backstitch (B'ST): For outlines and details, Backstitch should be worked after the design has been completed *(Fig. 6)*. When working over two fabric threads, work Backstitch as shown in **Fig. 7**.

Fig. 6   **Fig. 7**

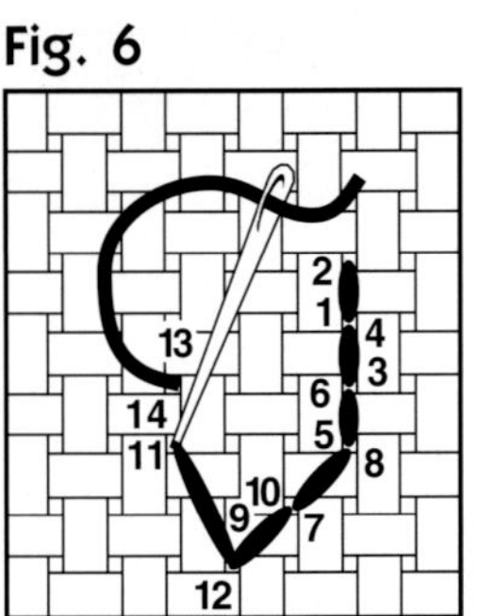
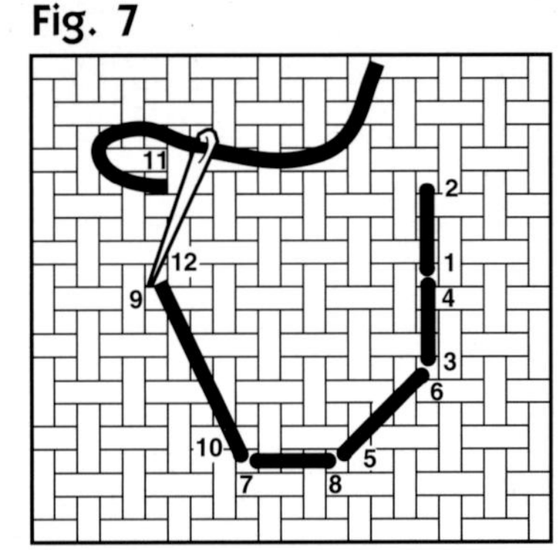

French Knot: Bring needle up at 1. Wrap floss once around needle. Insert needle at 2, tighten knot, and pull needle through fabric, holding floss until it must be released *(Fig. 8)*. For a larger knot, use more floss strands; wrap only once.

Fig. 8

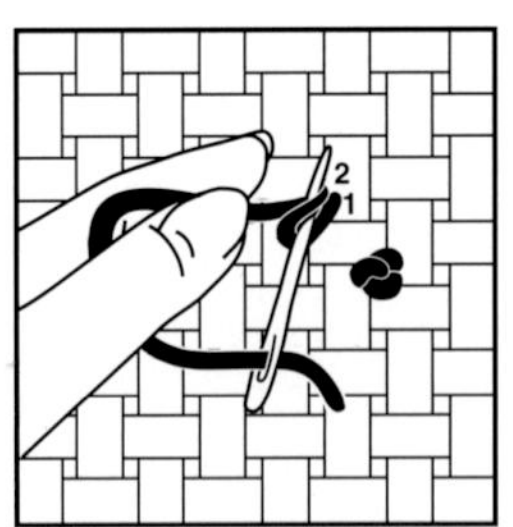

Stitching Tips

Preparing Fabric

Being sure to allow plenty of margin, cut fabric desired size and overcast raw edges. It is better to waste a little fabric than to come up short after hours of stitching!

Working with Floss

To ensure smoother stitches, separate strands and realign them before threading needle. Keep stitching tension consistent. Begin and end floss by running under several stitches on back; never tie knots.

Dye Lot Variation

It is important to buy all of the floss you need to complete your project from the same dye lot. Although variations in color may be slight when flosses from two different dye lots are held together, the variation is usually apparent on a stitched piece.

Where to Start

The horizontal and vertical centers of each charted design are shown by arrows. You may start at any point on the charted design, but be sure the design will be centered on the fabric. Locate the center of fabric by folding in half, top to bottom and again left to right. On the charted design, count the number of squares (stitches) from the center of the chart to where you wish to start. Then from the fabric's center, find your starting point by counting out the same number of fabric threads (stitches). *(To work over two fabric threads, count out twice the number of fabric threads.)*

Working over Two Fabric Threads

When working over two fabric threads, the stitches should be placed so that vertical fabric threads support each stitch. Make sure that the first Cross Stitch is placed on the fabric with stitch 1-2 beginning and ending where a vertical fabric thread crosses over a horizontal fabric thread *(Fig. 9)*.

Fig. 9

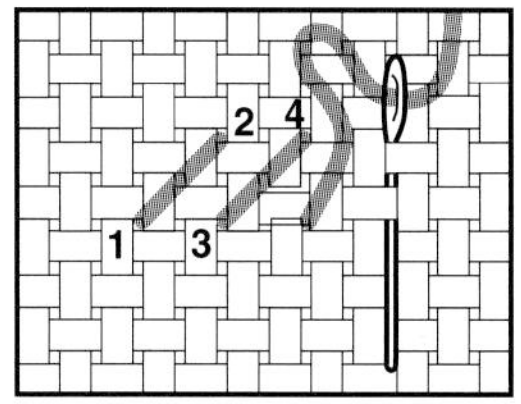

Finishing Techniques

Afghan Preparation

1. Cut off selvages. Fabric should measure 45"w x 58"l. Measure 5½" from raw edge of fabric and pull out one fabric thread. Fringe fabric up to missing thread. Repeat for each side. Tie an overhand knot at each corner with 4 horizontal and 4 vertical fabric threads. Working from corners, use 8 fabric threads for each knot until all threads are knotted.

2. Refer to afghan diagram for placement of design.

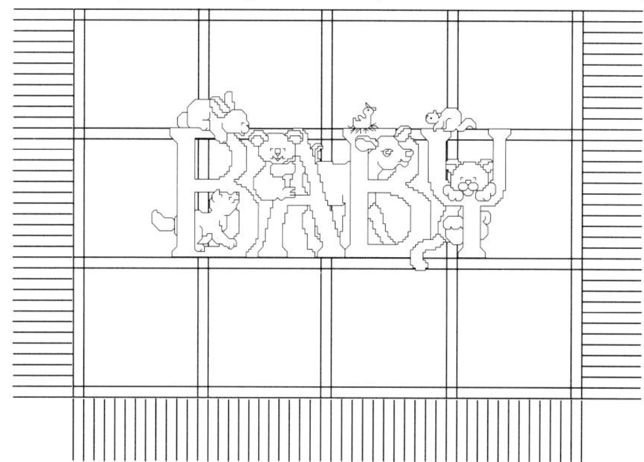

Making a Pillow

When sewing, match right sides and raw edges and use a ¹/₂" seam allowance.

1. Trim stitched piece to desired finished size plus ½" on all sides for seam allowances.

2. Cut the following: backing — one fabric piece same size as pillow front; ¼" diameter cord — one length same measurement as outer edge of pillow front plus 3"; cording fabric — one 2" wide bias strip same length as cord; ruffle — one fabric strip two times the desired finished width plus 1" for seam allowances and two times the measurement of the outer edge of pillow front.

3. Center cord on wrong side of cording fabric. Matching long edges, fold cording fabric over cord. Gently stretching fabric as you sew, use zipper foot to baste next to cord.

4. Beginning 1" from one end, baste cording to pillow front, clipping seam allowances at corners to allow cording to lie flat. Leaving needle in fabric, cut off one end of cording so it overlaps the other end by 1". Remove 1" of stitching from loose end of cording. Holding fabric away from cord, cut cord so ends butt together. Fold loose end of fabric under ½", lap it around other end, and continue stitching cording to pillow front.

5. Sew ends of ruffle together; press seam allowances open. With wrong sides together, press ruffle in half. To gather ruffle, baste ³/₈" and ¼" from raw edges. Pull basting threads, gathering ruffle to fit edge of pillow front. Baste ruffle to pillow front over cording.

6. Use zipper foot to sew pillow front and backing together as close as possible to cording, leaving an opening for turning. Trim corners diagonally, turn right side out, and press. Stuff with polyester fiberfill; slipstitch opening closed.

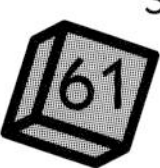

Making a Door Pillow

When sewing, match right sides and raw edges and use a 1/2" seam allowance.

1. Trim stitched piece to desired finished size plus 1/2" on all sides for seam allowances.

2. Cut the following: backing — one fabric piece same size as pillow front; 1/4" diameter cord — one length same measurement as outer edge of pillow front plus 3"; cording fabric — one 2" wide bias strip same length as cord.

3. Center cord on wrong side of cording fabric. Matching long edges, fold cording fabric over cord. Gently stretching fabric as you sew, use zipper foot to baste next to cord.

4. Beginning 1" from one end, baste cording to pillow front, clipping seam allowances at corners to allow cording to lie flat. Leaving needle in fabric, cut off one end of cording so it overlaps the other end by 1". Remove 1" of stitching from loose end of cording. Holding fabric away from cord, cut cord so ends butt together. Fold loose end of fabric under 1/2", lap it around other end, and continue stitching cording to pillow front.

5. Use zipper foot to sew pillow front and backing together as close as possible to cording, leaving an opening for turning. Trim corners diagonally, turn right side out, and press. Stuff with polyester fiberfill; slipstitch opening closed.

6. For hanger, cut one 10" length of ribbon. Attach one end to top of pillow front at each corner. Cut two 8" lengths of ribbon and tie in a bow. Attach each bow over ribbon ends on pillow front.

Making a Wall Hanging (Two Little Eyes)

When sewing, match right sides and raw edges and use a 1/4" seam allowance. Press all seam allowances in one direction.

1. Centering design, trim stitched piece to 12 1/2" x 20 1/2".

2. Cut fifty-two 2" x 4" strips from assorted fabrics.

3. Matching long edges, sew eight strips together for each top and bottom border. Sew borders to top and bottom of stitched piece.

4. Sew eighteen fabric strips together for each side border. Sew side borders to stitched piece and attached borders.

5. Cut one piece of backing fabric and one piece of batting same size as wall hanging front. Layer batting, backing (right side up), and wall hanging front (wrong side up). Sew layers together leaving an opening at bottom edge. Clip seam allowances at corners. Turn wall hanging right side out, carefully pushing corners outward. Slipstitch opening closed.

6. For hanging sleeve, cut an 18" x 3" strip of fabric. Press edges 1/4" to wrong side; press edges 1/4" to wrong side again. Machine stitch pressed edges in place. Center hanging sleeve on back of wall hanging 1/4" from top edge. Slipstitch long edges in place, leaving ends open for hanging rod.

Making a Wall Hanging (Gardening Bunnies)

When sewing, match right sides and raw edges and use a 1/2" seam allowance unless noted.

1. Centering design, trim stitched piece to desired finished size plus 1/2" on all sides for seam allowances.

2. For inner borders, cut two 2"w fabric strips the same length as top edge of stitched piece. Sew to top and bottom edges of stitched piece. Cut two 2"w fabric strips the same length as side edges of stitched piece plus attached strips. Sew to side edges of stitched piece.

3. For outer borders, cut two 4"w fabric strips the same length as top and bottom edges of stitched piece plus attached strips. Sew to top and bottom of attached strips. Cut two 4"w fabric strips the same length as side edges of stitched piece plus attached strips. Sew to side edges of attached strips.

4. Cut one piece of backing fabric and one piece of batting same size as wall hanging front. Layer backing (wrong side up), batting, and wall hanging (right side up). Baste layers together.

5. Cut a 2 1/4"w bias strip of fabric the same length as the outer edge of the wall hanging plus 5". Press one end and one long edge 1/2" to the wrong side. Beginning with pressed end, pin unpressed edge of binding to wall hanging front. Sew binding in place, stitching through all layers. Fold pressed side of binding over to back of wall hanging and slipstitch in place.

6. For hanging sleeve, cut a 3"w piece of backing fabric 1" shorter than width of wall hanging. Press edges 1/2" to wrong side. Center hanging sleeve on back of wall hanging 3/4" from top edge. Slipstitch long edges in place leaving ends open for hanging rod.

Adding a Photo

Measure photo area to ensure desired photo will fit. Trim photo area along stitches being careful not to clip any stitches. Position and mount photo to back of stitched piece using craft glue or double-sided tape.

Project Information
Front Cover

Welcome Baby — stitched on an 18" x 16" piece of 14 count White Aida (design size 12" x 9$5/8$"; chart pgs. 56-59). Two strands of floss were used for Cross Stitch and 1 strand for Backstitch and French Knots. It was custom framed.

Babies are for Hugging — stitched on a prefinished hooded bath towel with a 14 count White Aida insert (design size 4$1/2$" x 4$3/4$"; chart pg. 45). Three strands of floss were used for Cross Stitch and 1 strand for Backstitch.

Pat-A-Cake — stitched on a 12" x 10" piece of 14 count White Aida (design size 6" x 4"; chart pg. 49). Two strands of floss were used for Cross Stitch and 1 strand for Backstitch. It was custom framed.

I Love Mommy — stitched on a prefinished 14 count White Aida bib (design size 3$5/8$" x 2$5/8$"; chart pg. 18). Three strands of floss were used for Cross Stitch and 1 strand for Backstitch.

Baby Sweet Baby — stitched on a prefinished hooded bath towel with a 14 count White Aida insert (design size 4$7/8$" x 4"; chart pg. 45). Three strands of floss were used for Cross Stitch and 1 strand for Backstitch.

Twinkle, Twinkle — stitched on a 12" x 10$1/2$" piece of 14 count White Aida (design size 6" x 4$1/4$"; chart pg. 48). Two strands of floss were used for Cross Stitch and 1 strand for Backstitch and French Knots. It was custom framed.

Back Cover

Now I Lay Me Down to Rest — stitched on a 12$1/2$" x 14" piece of 14 count White Aida (design size 6$3/8$" x 7$7/8$"; chart pgs. 32-33). Three strands of floss were used for Cross Stitch and 1 strand of floss or metallic thread for Backstitch and French Knots. See Making a Pillow, pg. 61.

Babies — stitched on a 14$1/2$" x 16$1/2$" piece of 14 count White Aida (design size 8$3/8$" x 10$3/8$"; chart pgs. 20-21). Three strands of floss were used for Cross Stitch and 1 strand for Backstitch and French Knots. It was custom framed.

Gardening Bunnies — stitched on an 18$1/2$" x 15" piece of 14 count White Aida (design size 12$1/8$" x 9"; chart pgs. 50-51). Two strands of floss were used for Cross Stitch and 1 strand for Backstitch and French Knots. See Making a Wall Hanging, pg. 62.

Page 2

A, B, C — individual letters stitched on 14 count White Aida (chart pgs. 40-44). Three strands of floss were used for Cross Stitch and 1 strand for Backstitch and French Knots.

A Gift from God — stitched on a 15" x 20" piece of 14 count White Aida (design size 8$5/8$" x 13$1/2$"; chart pgs. 36-37). Three strands of floss were used for Cross Stitch and 1 strand for Backstitch. It was custom framed.

Noah's Ark — stitched on a 14" x 14" piece of 14 count White Aida (design size 7$1/2$" x 7$5/8$"; chart pgs. 34-35). Three strands of floss were used for Cross Stitch and 1 strand for Backstitch and French Knots. See Making a Pillow, pg. 61.

Page 3

Two Little Eyes — stitched on a 15" x 23" piece of 18 count Antique White Aida over two fabric threads (design size 8$5/8$" x 16$7/8$"; chart pgs. 30-31). Six strands of floss were used for Cross Stitch and 2 strands for Backstitch except where noted in key. See Making a Wall Hanging, pg. 62.

Page 4

I See the Moon — stitched on a 9$1/2$" x 15" piece of 14 count White Aida (design size 3$3/8$" x 8$1/2$"; chart pg. 17). Three strands of floss were used for Cross Stitch and 1 strand for Backstitch. It was custom framed.

My Little Angel — stitched on a 14" x 16$1/2$" piece of 14 count White Aida (design size 8" x 10$1/8$"; chart pgs. 22-23). Three strands of floss were used for Cross Stitch and 1 strand of floss or metallic thread for Backstitch. It was custom framed.

Bear Photo Frame — stitched on a 13$1/2$" x 15$1/2$" piece of 14 count White Aida (design size 7$1/8$" x 9$1/4$"; chart pgs. 46-47). Two strands of floss were used for Cross Stitch and 1 strand for Backstitch and French Knots except where noted in key. It was custom framed. See Adding a Photo, pg. 62.

My Guardian Angel — stitched on an 11$1/2$" x 10$1/2$" piece of 14 count White Aida (design size 5$1/4$" x 4$1/4$"; chart pg. 16). Three strands of floss were used for Cross Stitch and 1 strand for Backstitch. See Making a Door Pillow, pg. 62.

Page 5

Matthew, Mark, Luke, and John — stitched on a 13" x 14" piece of 14 count Antique White Aida (design size 6³/₄" x 7¹/₂"; chart pgs. 28-29). Three strands of floss were used for Cross Stitch and 1 strand of floss or metallic thread for Backstitch except where noted in key. It was custom framed.

Bath 5¢ — stitched on a prefinished hooded bath towel with a 14 count White Aida insert (design size 9³/₄" x 6¹/₂"; chart pg. 39). Three strands of floss were used for Cross Stitch and 1 strand for Backstitch.

Bath 10¢ — stitched on a prefinished wash mitt with a 14 count White Aida insert (design size 4¹/₂" x 1⁷/₈"; chart pg. 38). Three strands of floss were used for Cross Stitch and 1 strand for Backstitch and French Knots.

Page 6

Help Us, Father — stitched on a 14" x 12¹/₂" piece of 14 count Antique White Aida (design size 8" x 6¹/₄"; chart pgs. 26-27). Three strands of floss were used for Cross Stitch and 1 strand for Backstitch and French Knots. It was custom framed.

Heavenly Bunnies — stitched on a 16¹/₂" x 19" piece of 14 count White Aida (design size 10³/₈" x 13"; chart pgs. 52-55). Two strands of floss were used for Cross Stitch and 1 strand for Backstitch except where noted in key. It was custom framed.

Hide 'N' Seek — stitched on an 18 count White All-Cotton Anne Cloth afghan over two fabric threads (design size 16" x 7³/₄"; chart pags. 24-25). Six strands of floss were used for Cross Stitch and 2 strands for Backstitch and French Knots. See Afghan Preparation, pg. 61.

Page 7

All designs were stitched on 14 count bibs using 3 strands of floss for Cross Stitch and 1 strand for Backstitch.

I Love Daddy (design size 3³/₄" x 2"; chart pg. 18)
I Love Grandma (design size 3⁷/₈" x 1⁷/₈"; chart pg. 19)
I Love Grandpa (design size 3⁵/₈" x 2³/₄"; chart pg. 19)
Hug Me (design size 7¹/₈" x 2¹/₄"; chart pg. 13)
Peek-A-Boo (design size 8⁵/₈" x 1³/₄"; chart pg. 13)
BABY (design size 5⁷/₈" x 1⁷/₈"; chart pg. 16)
Cow (design size 8¹/₄" x 2¹/₈"; chart pg. 9)
Happy Birthday (design size 8" x 2"; chart pg. 12)
Little Angel (design size 8¹/₄" x 1⁷/₈"; chart pg. 14)
B is for BABY (design size 7¹/₈" x 1⁷/₈"; chart pg. 14)

Page 8

All designs were stitched on 14 count bibs using 3 strands of floss for Cross Stitch and 1 strand for Backstitch and French Knots.

Train (design size 7" x 1⁷/₈"; chart pg. 11)
Spaghetti (design size 6⁷/₈" x 2"; chart pg. 11)
I'm a Honey Bee (design size 8¹/₄" x 2"; chart pg. 15)
Eat Your Veggies (design size 7³/₈" x 2"; chart pg. 15)
Bunnies (design size 6¹/₄" x 1⁷/₈"; chart pg. 12)
Fruit (design size 7⁵/₈" x 2"; chart pg. 10)
Artist (design size 8¹/₂" x 2¹/₈"; chart pg. 10)
Bears (design size 9" x 1⁷/₈"; chart pg. 9)

Some fabric provided courtesy of Zweigart®.
Embroidery floss provided courtesy of The DMC Corporation.

We would like to recognize Viking Husqvarna Sewing Machine Company of Cleveland, Ohio, for providing the sewing machines used to make many of our projects.

We have made every effort to ensure that these instructions are accurate and complete. We cannot, however, be responsible for human error, typographical mistakes, or variations in individual work.

Production Team: Writer – Carolyn Breeding and Artist – Teresa Boyd.

Instructions tested and some cover items made by Lori Gilbert, Donna L. Overman, and Helen Stanton.